LITTLE BOOK OF

HMS VICTORY

Liam McCann

LITTLE BOOK OF

HMS
VICTORY

First published in the UK in 2015

© Demand Media Limited 2015

www.demand-media.co.uk

Printed and bound in Europe

ISBN 978-1-910540-12-1

Contents

Introduction

Since its founding in the 16th century, the Royal Navy is considered the oldest branch of Britain's armed forces and is often called the 'Senior Service'. Before then, Britain relied on a few ships built at the time of Alfred the Great (871-899AD), which were upgraded by future kings to protect the islands from Norse invaders. In the late 10th and early 11th centuries, King Ethelred the Unready realised the importance of having a fleet so he ordered an enormous number of ships to be built to fight the Danes.

In August 991, the Danish fleet arrived at Northey Island in Essex, and the two sides fought a pitched land battle at Maldon. The English army was outnumbered and the Danes scored the first of several crushing defeats. They then extracted a monetary tribute from the natives under the pretence that it would protect the islanders from further attack, but the Danes immediately went back on their word and sent ships marauding up and down the Channel coast and into the Thames Estuary.

When King Sweyn launched yet another successful invasion in 1013, he decided to maintain a protective fleet via taxation, but this practice died out after the Norman Conquest and English naval power soon declined. For the next two centuries, the British fleet consisted solely of merchant ships that could be transformed into troop transports in times of war. The islands were well governed by subsequent monarchs and the threat from the continent faded, but, at

RIGHT King Ethelred the Unready was the first British monarch to realise the importance of maintaining a navy

the renewal of hostilities with the French at the beginning of the Hundred Years' War in 1337, a navy became a priority.

King Edward III destroyed the French fleet at the Battle of Sluys in 1340, but the major battles of the conflict were then confined to French soil. The English fleet was expanded to supply troops in Normandy so that they could continue operations against the old enemy. Some French raids did get through to England's ports on the south coast however, so the fleet was beefed up during the reign of Henry V.

Although the Hundred Years' War officially ended in 1453, subsequent monarchs believed a strong navy could be useful in combat as well as a deterrent. Henry VIII appointed a secretariat to oversee the dockyards and the building of dedicated warships throughout the 15th century, a move that paid dividends in the reign of Elizabeth I during England's ongoing war with the Spanish.

A number of privateers accompanied the fledgling navy's marauders in hunting treasure-laden Spanish galleons returning from South America, but it was only a matter of time before the Spanish countered. In 1588, Philip II ordered

RIGHT Philip II of Spain

FAR RIGHT Jean Froissart's depiction of the Battle of Sluys in 1340

his armada to destroy the British and Dutch fleets. The British had anticipated the Spanish retaliation, however, and they'd been preparing to repel an offensive for more than two years.

It was still customary for the crown to commandeer merchant ships and those in the hands of wealthy privateers. In 1586, Sir Walter Raleigh ordered a ship that, as was tradition, would bear the prefix 'Ark' and then his surname, thus *Ark Raleigh*. Plans for this galleon were submitted to the shipbuilder R. Chapman of Deptford and the 103-foot 800-ton ship was launched the following year. She was a formidable opponent with four 60-pound guns, four 30 pounders, twelve 18 pounders and 9 pounders, six 6 pounders and 17 smallbore weapons spread across two gun decks, a double forecastle, a quarterdeck and a poop deck. She was also a useful troop transport with room for 100 soldiers among her complement of 268 sailors and 32 gunners.

Raleigh, of course, had his sights set on plundering the galleons crossing the Atlantic for personal gain but Elizabeth I, fearing reprisals from Philip, bought the ship for £5,000 (which was deducted from Raleigh's tax bill). The ship was then handed over to her new commander, Lord High Admiral Charles Howard, First Earl of Nottingham, and renamed *Ark Royal*. The fleet at last had a flagship, and the name would live on for more than four hundred years.

The defeat of the Spanish Armada boosted British morale and gave the navy an aura of invincibility. However, slaving raids by the Barbary Corsairs (pirates operating out of North Africa) in the early 17th century dispelled both the myth and the navy's credibility. Charles I gave the service a boost by building a fleet of small but powerful warships, but he could only pay for them by increasing taxes, a strategy that led to national unrest and the outbreak of the English Civil War.

With Charles I having been executed and the monarchy abolished, Britain was seen as a soft target. Oliver Cromwell immediately expanded the navy to deter the French from invading and within a decade it was the most powerful in the world. British naval tactics were then refined so that the fleet would draw up in a line opposite the enemy so that they could engage all their broadside guns.

In 1651, the British limited trade with the Netherlands under the Navigation Act because they felt threatened by the

Dutch navy. The act prevented Dutch ships transporting British goods, so it targeted their economy and allowed the British merchant fleet to grow. The Dutch retaliated the following year by engaging the Royal Navy in the first of three sea battles. By then, however, there had been a shift in British shipbuilding towards much larger vessels that were designed to overpower enemy ships.

Cromwell was an experienced land campaigner but he was inexperienced in naval warfare so he asked Robert Blake and George Monk to devise a strategy for ensuring naval supremacy. Blake and Monk initially suggested allying with the Dutch so that the two great sea powers could defeat the Franco-Spanish alliance and conquer America. The Dutch saw this as an attempt to end their sovereignty, however, and dismissed the English offer. Cromwell was deeply offended and de-cided to confront the Dutch in battle.

Blake and Monk then came up with a

paper instructing captains how to fight sea battles, with the emphasis remaining on a linear broadside-to-broadside action. This allowed the admiral's signals from the flagship to be passed along the line, hence the term 'ships-of-the-line'. These tactics invariably led to ships being fitted with more cannon as broadside firepower was the decisive element. The largest ships became known as first-raters and they were often around 150 feet in length with more than 100 cannon spread over three decks. These leviathans took between three and five years to build from 4,000 tons of prime timber, so they were costly in terms of time, money and workforce (at least 1,000 men worked on the 102-gun *Sovereign of the Seas* before her launch in 1637).

The British insisted that all foreign ships strike their flags (meaning lower them in deference to the greater power) on encountering a vessel of the Royal Navy, but Lieutenant-Admiral Maarten Tromp refused to acknowledge Admiral Blake's fleet in May 1652 so the two sides finally lined up at the Battle of Goodwin Sands. It was a minor skirmish where both fleets suffered little damage but Cromwell saw it as a slight and the Commonwealth declared war on the Dutch in July.

Both sides scored victories over the next two years, but, with the restoration of the monarchy under Charles II, the fleet was again laid up due to lack of funds. The Dutch saw an opening in the English defences and ruthlessly exploited it, sailing up the River Medway to Chatham Docks in 1667 and burning the majority of the fleet at anchor. It was perhaps the most crushing defeat in the history of the navy. The English immediately allied with the French to counter this new threat but the Dutch were well drilled and they repelled every attack during the third Anglo-Dutch War (1672-74).

Under Chief Secretary to the Admiralty Samuel Pepys, the navy became more professional and better drilled. With greater power came greater responsibility and the fleet soon ended the threat from the Barbary Corsairs and forced the North African states to accept favourable peace treaties with England. The navy's attention then turned back to France, and, in an alliance with the Dutch, the English scored victories that would see them dominate the waves for the next 100 years.

During the late 17th century, the

LEFT A contemporary engraving of HMS Sovereign of the Seas

navy lobbied for government funds to build dedicated warships. Crews were then recruited and trained to the highest standards of seamanship and combat. A class system based on officers of varying ranks and ordinary seamen was also established. This newly modernised navy, with its superior tactics and organisation, high standards of hygiene, extensive dockyard facilities, excellent logistical support and first-rate ship design was the first professional military force in the world. When the Act of the Union united England and Scotland in 1707, the ships of both navies combined to form the Royal Navy of Great Britain.

For the next 200 years, the navy was the most powerful in the world, although it was occasionally outnumbered, such as when French marauders captured British and Dutch convoys in the Mediterranean. The Royal Navy's retaliation was emphatic and lasting, however: they destroyed the entire French fleet in the Mediterranean at the Battle of Toulon in 1707, and there were more victories over the Spanish when they tried to take the British-held territories of Gibraltar and Menorca.

Despite its size and superiority, the Royal Navy was expected to police trouble spots across the globe so it was often spread too thinly. It failed to break through the French blockade at the Battle of Chesapeake in the American Revolutionary War so Britain could no longer support the colonial rebels. This led to their surrender at Yorktown, which effectively ended British involvement in North America.

When the introduction of lemons and other fresh vegetables finally eradicated scurvy in the late 18th century, British naval power was restored (the disease reportedly killed 130,000 of the 190,000 sailors conscripted during the Seven Years' War with the French between 1755 and 1763). Commanders like Horatio Nelson then ensured its supremacy for another hundred years. By the dawn of the 19th century, the British fleet boasted 600 cruisers, more than the rest of the world's navies combined.

A second engagement at Toulon in 1793 saw an enormous French fleet destroyed. The Spanish and Dutch then joined forces with the remains of the French navy but they too were routed at the Battle of Camperdown in 1797. And Napoleon's army in Egypt was left isolated after Nelson annihilated his fleet at the Battle of the Nile the following year. Britain proved her dominance by crushing

a Danish force at the Battle of Copenhagen in 1801.

The Royal Navy's defining moment came at Trafalgar in 1805, however. Thirty-three British ships faced off against 41 ships of the combined French and Spanish navies off the southwest coast of Spain. Nelson shunned conventional naval tactics, which dictated lining your fleet up opposite the enemy and then trying to pound them into submission. Instead, he divided his ships into two lines and drove them through the opposition at right angles in a manoeuvre known as crossing the T. It gave the French and Spanish an early advantage in that their ships could train all their portside guns at the Royal Navy but, as soon as their battle line had been crossed, Nelson opened up from both flanks and tore into the French fleet. They lost 22 ships and 14,000 men, while Nelson lost no ships and little more than 1,000 men. It was such a decisive engagement that it secured British naval supremacy until the middle of the 20th century.

Nelson's flagship at the battle was HMS *Victory*.

Chapter 1

The Story of HMS Victory

Britain was at war with France and Spain for much of the 18th century so there was always a demand for capital ships. However, the navy only commissioned 10 during this turbulent period.

Surveyor of the Navy Sir Thomas Slade was the architect tasked with designing and building a new first-rate ship (the naval designation for the largest ships of the line) in July 1758. He based his design on HMS *Royal George*, which had been commissioned in 1746 and launched 10 years later. He also measured captured French ships to examine their technology and assess whether it could be improved. The layout of their sails and design of their hulls, for

example, might yield an extra couple of knots. Any such speed advantage could be crucial in battle.

At 227 feet, his latest ship would be eight feet longer but otherwise comparable with the *Royal George* in tonnage and armament: approximately 2,100 tons burthen and carrying 100 guns. Her keel was made from seven large elm trees

and laid in the old single dock exactly a year after Slade's proposal had been accepted. A kilometre of fir and spruce was then used for the decks, masts and yard arms as it was more flexible than oak and wouldn't splinter in heavy seas. The lower masts were then made from up to seven trees bound inside iron hoops. The hull below the water-

LEFT Sir Thomas Slade designed the Victory and based her on HMS Royal George

ABOVE John Christian Schetky's painting depicting the loss of the Royal George

line was eventually covered with 3,923 four-foot by one-foot copper plates weighing 17 tons. This was to aid manoeuvrability and protect against the teredo worm.

Her name wasn't chosen until 1760 but *Victory* clearly referenced the balance of power in the ongoing Seven Years' War. The previous year, the British had won overwhelming land victories at Quebec in Canada and Minden in what was Prussia but which is now Germany. It became known as the Year of Victories when the navy also defeated the French at the Battle of Lagos off the coast of Portugal and at the Battle of Quiberon Bay near Saint Nazaire. With the French and British vying for control of the wood and fur trade in Canada, as well as sugar resources in the Caribbean, there would be more conflict between the two over the next half century.

The war involved the major European powers and raged until the treaties of Saint Petersburg and Hamburg (1762), then Paris and Hubertusburg (1763) saw Britain strip France of all its land in the eastern half of North America. France also lost the Northern Circars in India, while Spain ceded

Florida to Britain.

Several senior officers lobbied to use a different name for the new ship because the previous incarnation of *Victory* had been lost with all hands when she was wrecked in the English Channel in 1744. The name wasn't in use, however, and the three other ships that had been named *Victory* had distinguished service careers.

The first was a 42-gun ship that was commissioned in 1569 and broken up in 1608. The second was a great ship that was converted into a second-rate ship and remained with the navy from 1620 until 1691. During her career, she fought in the attack on La Rochelle in 1627 as well as another 11 major sea battles. The third incarnation had been launched as HMS *Royal James* in 1675 but was renamed *Victory* in 1691. She was a first-rate ship-of-the-line with 100 cannon that saw action in the Battle of Barfleur. Although she was partly destroyed by fire in 1721, most of her timber went into the fourth HMS *Victory*. This ship wasn't so lucky, however. She foundered during a storm in 1744 and her remains weren't discovered until 2008.

The new ship's frame was complete by the end of 1760, after which it was usual

LEFT The sinking of the previous HMS Victory in 1744

RIGHT The Great Cabin

to cover the hull and leave the wood to season for a few months (more than 5,000 oak trees and several hundred each of elm, pine and fir went into her construction). The 300,000 cubic feet of wood used during the build came from 100 acres of forest and could have covered the Empire State Building and Canary Wharf. The war was effectively over by then, however, so work was suspended on *Victory* until 1763. Her hull wasn't finished for another two years but she was eventually launched on May 7, 1765. She was found to have a significant list to starboard and was immediately towed away to have it corrected with 34 tons of shingle ballast.

The ship was designed as the navy's flagship so she had to cater for the admiral of the fleet as well as the captain. Conditions in the Great Cabin, which occupied a quarter of the upper gun deck, were luxurious when compared with the rest of the ship but the cabin was prone to violent motion during heavy seas and damp during adverse weather. The cabin was divided into four areas: the day cabin doubled as an office where the commander outlined his strategy (the seats and bulkheads concealed hidden gun-ports and even private toilets); the dining cabin was used for entertaining senior officers and guests; the steerage ante room was home to valets and secretaries; and the bed place held the admiral's bunk (mounted between two 12-pound cannon).

Victory's orlop deck was below the waterline but her hull was three feet thick so there was no need for extra armour that would have weighed her down and made her sluggish in light winds. She was then fitted out with thirty 42-pound smoothbore cast-iron cannon on her lower gun-deck (amounting to 110 tons of iron), twenty-eight 24-pounders on her middle deck and thirty 12-pounders on her upper deck. She also had 12 six-pounders mounted on her quarterdeck and forecastle.

All *Victory*'s guns were smoothbore muzzle-loaders with an effective range of up to a mile. They fired three types of shot: round shot was used to penetrate the hulls of enemy ships; dismantling shot was fired at the rigging to cripple the opposing vessel; and grape shot was designed to kill or maim the enemy crew. (*Victory* carried more firepower than Wellington had at his disposal at Waterloo in 1815.) The gun-deck would be home for 350 men throughout her service life. They ate, slept and fought in cramped conditions amongst the cannon.

FAR LEFT The dining cabin was used to entertain officers and distinguished guests

LEFT The master's bunk

FAR LEFT The lower gun deck bristles with cannon

LEFT The 32-pound smoothbore cannon

Victory also had three enormous masts and a bowsprit, giving her a ship-rigged configuration. The foremast reached 182 feet, the mainmast 205 feet and the mizzenmast 152 feet. Her 37 vast sails occupied an area of nearly 7,000 square yards (approximately the same as a football pitch) and gave her a top speed of around nine knots. To run the ship, 26 miles of flax and hemp rope plus 1,000 wooden tackle blocks were needed for the rigging alone, while another 800 blocks were required for the guns. The largest of these ropes was 19 inches in circumference.

Her elaborate figurehead had two cupids supporting the royal coat of arms and the crown. The inscription Honi Soit Qui Mal Y Pense was taken from the Order of the Garter and means 'shame to him who evil thinks'. Her 30-foot sternpost would bear enormous stresses at sea, particularly in bad weather, so it was built from a single oak tree. Other trees with so-called 'compass timbers' were chosen for the wing transoms. The remaining wood had to be bent to the correct size and shape over fire-pits. The pieces were then doused with water and weighted until they reached the correct curvature.

Victory carried six boats as part of her equipment: a launch, one barge, a pinnace,

two 25-foot cutters and one 18-foot cutter. They were used primarily to ferry stores and men around the harbour or occasionally to tow the ship in calm weather. The launch was 34 feet long and was mainly used for anchor work so it was fitted with a windlass and small wooden crane. (All the boats were used to launch covert attacks on enemy ships and shore positions so they were towed astern in battle to prevent them taking collateral damage.)

Victory carried seven anchors, two of which weighed more than four tons each. They were used to secure the ship in deep water and were usually stored on the starboard side because of the prevailing winds in the northern hemisphere. The anchors had to be raised and lowered manually using two capstans in the centre of the ship. Each was manned by up to 72 men. The six-inch diameter cable had to be stored in a dry but aerated locker to prevent it from rotting.

Despite the expense and labour that went into her construction, *Victory* immediately ran the risk of becoming an

LEFT Victory's magazine

ABOVE The quarterdeck

FAR LEFT HMS
Victory's bow and
figurehead

LEFT The Victory's
complex rigging

expensive white elephant (she cost more than £50 million to build in today's currency). Britain was no longer at war so she was dis-masted, covered and listed as a reserve ship while moored in the River Medway. Indeed, she wasn't commissioned until France joined the American War of Independence in 1778.

The British had expanded the empire throughout North America so they then had to raise taxes to manage the colonies. The French saw an opportunity to side with the revolutionaries against the British and joined the war. Britain responded to the threat by turning to the navy.

Captain John Lindsay was initially given command of *Victory* but he was soon transferred to the *Prince George*. Admiral Augustus Keppel was then placed in charge of the Channel Fleet. He chose *Victory* as his flagship and installed Captain John Campbell as her master. His second in command was Jonathan Faulknor. Campbell insisted the 42-pounders were swapped for 32-pounders but this decision was reversed in 1779. A vast quantity of stores and provisions were then loaded aboard: 360 tons of water, 50 tons of beer, 45 tons of salted meat and the same of bread or biscuits, plus two tons of peas, two of but-

ter and 10 tons of flower. Logistically, the operation was as complex as it is to stock a cruiser liner today.

Her crew were highly skilled. Most would have come from a captain's previous command, while a smaller proportion would be criminals doing military service rather than spending their lives in jail. Very few would have been 'impressed', although it was more common in times of war or hardship when volunteers were in short supply.

The class system was adhered to onboard, with the captain and officers enjoying privileged surroundings and the finest fare. Life for ordinary seaman was tough and uncompromising, however. They were worked extremely hard and had to survive on meagre rations. Living conditions were also cramped and uncomfortable (the hammocks were only 14 inches wide) but for most this was actually preferable to their circumstances ashore: the state needed these men to be in prime physical and mental condition so they were fed three times a day (with occasional portions of meat) and were allowed the odd tot of rum or ration of beer. Hot meals could only be prepared in the galley in calm weather so these were rare, and fresh vegetables were

an infrequent luxury. The food may have been monotonous but it was nutritious and provided more than 4,000 calories per day. The average in the 21st century is around 2,500 calories so the crews were clearly worked hard.

The ship's surgeon was perhaps the most important member of the crew: he had to deal with minor ailments from boils and burns to malnutrition, tropical diseases and horrific battle wounds. Other than traditional cures, sailors were also allowed beer and diluted rum (grog) to ease their pain. The rum ration was actually so large that most sailors were in a perpetual state of mild inebriation. And beer was usually safer to drink than water (the brewing process killed bacteria and other harmful organisms). Indeed, the alcohol ration is often credited with boosting morale and allowing captains to maintain discipline, two of the most important aspects of naval warfare.

There were frequent breaches of discipline, however, and punishment was usually swift and harsh. However, at a time when the penalty for stealing on land was death by hanging, the navy is also credited with gradually reducing sentences for offences. Most crimes aboard ship were punished by flogging.

Each crewman's routine was governed by their watches, during which they set and trimmed the sails and helped navigate the ship. The junior seamen weren't allocated watches and were tasked with cleaning the ship with sandstone blocks at 5.30am instead. The crew also had to practise their gunnery skills. Six men manned each cannon: the number one was the gun captain who was responsible for aiming and firing; numbers two and five were spikers who turned and raised or lowered the barrel; the number three loaded the gun and rammed the shot and powder home; number four was a sponger who checked the barrel for any impurities that might cause the charge to ignite prematurely; and number sixes were usually boys in their early teens who collected the powder charges from the magazines deeper in the hold.

Victory's gun crews were so highly trained that they could fire and reload in just 90 seconds, but it was such a finely honed skill that if any one of the crew failed, the gun would become obsolete and the system broke down. Just months after being launched, they would be tested for the first time.

Victory was now ready for battle.

LEFT
The portside anchor

Chapter 2

Action Stations!

RIGHT Comte Louis
Guilloumet d'Orvilliers

FAR RIGHT An artist's
rendition of Victory in
Portsmouth

HMS *Victory* put to sea from Spithead in the summer of 1778. France had joined the American War of Independence earlier that year and their fleet of 30 ships-of-the-line and two naval auxiliaries under the command of Comte Louis Guilloumet (d'Orvilliers) put out from Brest on July 8 to monitor the British fleet. Although d'Orvilliers had orders to retreat rather than engage if the two came together, the British force of 29 ships-of-the-line cornered his fleet 100 miles off the island of Ushant at the mouth of the English Channel.

D'Orvilliers had the more favourable weather so he dispatched two ships back to port. He then tried to outmanoeuvre the British fleet in the hope that he could avoid the confrontation. However, the

weather then turned and scattered his ships while the British maintained their column. This game of nautical chess continued overnight as d'Orvilliers pressed to windward. In the morning, he found himself to the northwest of Keppel but this suited both men: Keppel was blocking the French retreat to Brest while d'Orvilliers had the weather-gage (the advantageous upwind position) and was keeping his promise to avoid engaging the enemy.

For the next four days, the wind continued to the west and d'Orvilliers managed to keep the British out of range. By the morning of July 27, the fleets had closed to within 10 miles but the southwesterly wind meant the British were soon giving a 'general chase', which allowed the fleet to break formation to engage the enemy.

At daybreak, Sir Hugh Palliser's rear squadron dropped astern of the French fleet and took up the chase. By nine o'clock, d'Orvilliers ordered his fleet to countermarch, which caused a loss of ground to leeward. The British then used a more southerly breeze to head directly for the French fleet. When it seemed as if they had no choice but to engage, a squall concealed the fleets from one an-

other until mid-morning, by which time the British had closed on the French rear quarter. D'Orvilliers desperately ordered his fleet to go about but several ships didn't acknowledge the order and the fleet was soon in disarray.

By resuming the port tack, the heads of the columns would meet on equal terms, but it took until nearly noon before the French column had re-formed. It was obvious to Keppel that d'Orvilliers had orders to run and would only fight if cornered so he continued stalking the enemy until his entire fleet was in position to join the action. Keppel then gave the order to fire before most of the ships were flying their colours. D'Orvilliers managed to gather his biggest ships and pass the British line to windward but *Victory* opened proceedings at noon by shelling *Bretagne* and then *Ville de Paris*.

The French had been outmanoeuvred but they still managed to advance on a parallel line four points off the wind. The leading three ships then hauled their wind to pull away from the British in a bid to defuse the engagement. The fourth French ship returned fire from close range but they were soon handicapped by smoke and had to cease firing in case they struck one of their own ships.

Palliser's flagship, *Formidable*, slowed to allow HMS *Ocean* and *Elizabeth* into the action but they almost ended up firing on one another in the confusion.

As soon as the 10 ships of the British van (lead squadron) had passed the French rear, Vice-Admiral Sir Robert Harland ordered the squadron about so they could give chase. By now the French column was running free so Keppel withdrew *Victory* to give his crew time to repair her rigging.

By two o'clock in the afternoon, *Victory* had come about and was also in pursuit of the French but Keppel was convinced the enemy was retreating and ordered the battle signal brought down. He then signalled for the fleet to re-form on the *Victory*'s weather bow but none of the centre division were in position to join the flagship. By 2.30pm, only three ships had formed up, while the rest milled about in confusion or were disabled.

When the smoke cleared, d'Orvilliers realised the British were in disarray so he ordered his fleet to line up for battle on the starboard tack. His first message didn't get through, however. The fourth ship from the van finally went about as d'Orvilliers explained that he wanted to pass alongside the disoriented British fleet. By going to

FAR LEFT John Wollaston's portrait of Augustus Keppel

LEFT Sir Hugh Palliser

FAR LEFT The First
Battle of Ushant by
Theodore Gudin

LEFT Luc Urbain du
Bouëxic, Comte de
Guichen

leeward, he could present his weather-side to the enemy. This would allow him to open his lower gun ports and fire his larger guns.

The fleet was slow to respond, however, and Keppel soon realised his intent. He was in the weaker position so he stood the *Victory* down and tacked towards his crippled ships, although he kept flying the battle signal so that his fleet maintained their readiness. Palliser saw this as a cowardly retreat, however, even though Keppel was simply allowing him to cover the rear and make repairs. The remaining ships then fell in line behind *Victory* and at four o'clock in the afternoon Harland's division were ready for battle once more. Palliser's squadron joined up at the rear of the *Formidable* as the captains took station from the divisional commander rather than from the *Victory*.

Formidable was now on the *Victory*'s weather quarter so she took the initiative. An hour later, Keppel asked Palliser to hasten into the line as he was waiting for him to renew the action now that the French had completed their manoeuvre and had drawn up in the lee of the British fleet. Harland was repositioned in the van but Palliser was trapped and couldn't move so Keppel refrained from summoning the

rear ships into line until 7pm, by which time it was too late to re-engage the enemy.

At daybreak the following morning, most of the French fleet had retreated 15 miles to the southeast and the battle was effectively over. The result was indecisive as the losses on both sides were similar: the British suffered 407 dead and 789 wounded, while the French lost 126 killed and 413 wounded.

Considering d'Orvilliers had been trying to avoid confrontation, his tactics of firing into the British fleet to disable

their ships had worked reasonably well. Keppel and Palliser had been forced to make running repairs and couldn't attack when they pleased. The French fleet may have taken more direct hits when they did finally engage, but they had also outmanoeuvred the British more than once.

Both sides claimed victory as a matter of honour. Had d'Orvilliers managed to pass by the British when they were in disarray, the outcome would have favoured the French, but the French commander

failed to seize the opportunity and gave the British time to make repairs. Keppel then failed to capitalise on poor French organisation. He wasted time manoeuvring and allowed the French to escape.

Although the engagement was indecisive, Keppel and Palliser disagreed about their tactics so strongly that the First Battle of Ushant became a national disgrace. Keppel maintained that Palliser wasn't ready for battle, while Palliser claimed he was awaiting orders to attack. The admiral was eventually court-martialled and cleared, while Palliser was heavily criticised by the subsequent inquiry. It was an unsatisfactory and embarrassing end to *Victory*'s first naval engagement.

Two years later, *Victory*'s hull was given a copper sheath below the waterline to protect it from shipworm. The following December, she put to sea with 12 other ships under the command of Rear-Admiral Richard Kempenfelt. His orders were to intercept a French convoy sailing with a cargo of supplies from Brest to their outposts in the West Indies.

Kempenfelt had no idea that the convoy was being guarded by 19 ships-of-the-line so it came as something of a surprise

when the French fleet was spotted on December 12. The Comte de Guichen was in the weaker downwind position, however, so he could do little to defend the convoy as the *Victory* swept through their ranks and helped capture 15 of the transport ships. Kempenfelt wisely chose to avoid confronting the escorts and a storm then scattered the remaining ships. Most returned to port, while only two

LEFT George Augustus Eliott by Joshua Reynolds

ABOVE The British destroy the floating batteries during the Siege of Gibraltar

RIGHT Admiral Richard Howe's relief of Gibraltar in 1782. HMS Victory is in the centre

ships-of-the-line and a couple of transports actually made it to the West Indies.

Attacking a much larger force was deemed so reckless that Kempenfelt's action was challenged in Parliament. An inquiry criticised the navy so severely that Lord Frederick North's government eventually collapsed.

Half a century earlier, Britain had considered ceding Gibraltar to the Spanish but, when the amenable King Ferdinand VI died in 1759, Charles III took a much tougher stance with the British. Two years later, Charles signed a family truce with Louis XV of France (with whom Britain were at war), so Britain responded by declaring war on Spain. Britain dominated the exchanges but there was a period of peace between 1763 and 1779. The French and Spanish had been waiting to avenge earlier defeats so they began supplying arms to the American rebels in the hope that British forces would be divided and weakened.

With the British occupied in North America, the French and Spanish could move into British-held Gibraltar and end their dominance in the Mediterranean. The Spanish navy immediately blockaded the territory and moved 13,000 troops into the area to the north to build forts and gun batteries. Eleven ships were then dispatched to the Gulf of Cádiz in case the British sent reinforcements. British forces in Gibraltar were commanded by Governor-General George Eliott and only numbered around 5,400 but he was an inspirational leader who mounted a determined defence.

By the winter of 1779, however, the British were low on supplies and their fuel was also exhausted. There was an outbreak of scurvy when their fresh vegetable stocks were depleted but they still maintained their defence of the rock. The Spanish were forced to commit more men to the siege and even postponed a planned invasion of Britain.

The Royal Navy sent Admiral George Rodney to the rescue. He captured a Spanish convoy in January 1780 and then took another four Spanish ships at the Battle of Cape St Vincent off Portugal the following week. He then broke through the blockade with 1,000 reinforcements and an abundance of supplies. As soon as Rodney had retreated, however, the Spanish resumed their siege and both sides exchanged gunfire throughout the summer.

By April the following year, the British were again in danger of losing the terri-

tory. Vice-Admiral George Darby ran the blockade with 130 ships but the Spanish were unable to intercept. Instead, they unleashed a terrific bombardment but only succeeded in destroying most of the town. Darby eventually rescued all the civilians and evaded the besieging navy during his escape.

The French and Spanish were left with no option but to invade the territory, but Eliott again proved his tactical nous by launching a counterattack before they were in position. His men routed the Spanish positions and withdrew to their forts before the Spanish could launch their strike. By September, however, the Spanish had regrouped and 5,000 men invaded on revolutionary floating batteries. They were supported by 70 ships and another 25,000 troops, plus 35,000 land troops. A civilian militia numbering around 75,000 then moved into the hills to the north.

The rock took a tremendous pounding but the British garrison retaliated with red-hot shot that sank or severely damaged 10 of the floating batteries, resulting in the loss of 700 men. The garrison then captured the 72-gun ship *San Miguel* when it was dis-masted in a storm. Captain Juan Moreno surrendered when it

eventually ran aground and the defenders captured nearly 700 men.

The admiralty eventually had to relieve the rock so Admiral Richard Howe was dispatched aboard HMS *Victory* in September 1782. He arrived off Cape St Vincent to discover the enemy fleet had been scattered in a storm so he entered Gibraltar unopposed. Sixty-five ships resupplied the rock with food and ammunition, and they also landed three infantry regiments.

Howe engaged the enemy fleet during his withdrawal at the Battle of Cape Spartel. Forty-nine French and Spanish ships under Admiral Luis de Córdova had been anchored in Algeciras Bay for a month but they were in poor condition after a storm had ripped through the fleet. Córdova could have attacked while the British were resupplying Gibraltar but he left it until Howe was making his escape.

On October 19, Howe reduced *Victory*'s sails and offered Córdova the chance to engage (his opposite number held the upwind position). Córdova gave the order to chase and his flagship, *Santísima Trinidad*, breached the British line the following afternoon. The Spanish front squadron opened fire but Howe reduced sail and fooled 15 Span-

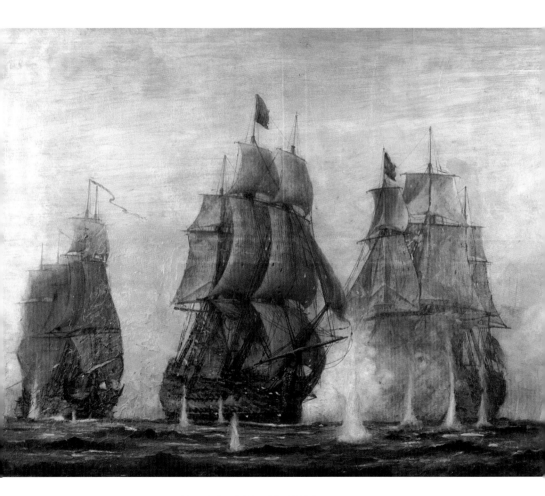

ish ships into ceding their weather advantage. Córdova maintained his pursuit but Howe outmanoeuvred the remaining fleet and completed his escape with the rest of the convoy. The coppering of the hulls made the Royal Navy's ships faster and more manoeuvrable, so Howe always held the upper hand. His primary goal of resupplying Gibraltar and escaping was achieved.

By 1783, the Treaty of Paris had ended the American Revolutionary War. French and Spanish troops stationed around Gibraltar had failed for nearly four years to break British resistance on the rock. George Eliott was made a Knight of the Bath in recognition of his outstanding service during the Great Siege. Although the peace treaty left Gibraltar in British hands, the empire was forced to concede Minorca in the Mediterranean and several territories in the West Indies to the Spanish.

There was an uneasy peace between the British and Spanish for the next decade but the two countries again came to blows during the French Revolutionary Wars (1792-1802). The 1796 Treaty of San Ildefonso allied the French and Spanish against the British so Britain immediately blockaded Spanish ports and cut off supply lines to their territories in North America. The Spanish responded by massing their Mediterranean fleet off Elba and Corsica, forcing the British to evacuate the islands.

In early February 1797, the bulk of the Spanish fleet under Don José de Córdoba then left Cartagena to join up with the French at Brest. Their secondary objective was to escort a merchant fleet to Cádiz. Before they reached the port, a strong easterly wind forced them into the Atlantic.

Admiral Sir John Jervis's British Mediterranean Fleet, meanwhile, sailed from Tagus in Portugal to intercept the Spanish. As he only commanded 10 ships-of-the-line, five more under Rear-Admiral William Parker were dispatched from the Channel Fleet as reinforcements.

Commodore Horatio Nelson aboard his frigate HMS *Minerve* then stumbled across the Spanish fleet on February 11. He manoeuvred amongst the enemy ships but avoided detection due to the thick fog. Nelson reached the rest of the British fleet two days later and instructed Jervis on the *Victory* where to find the Spanish. Despite not knowing the size of the enemy fleet, Jervis sailed immediately

LEFT The Battle of Cape St Vincent

ABOVE Nelson's HMS Captain captures the San Nicolas and San Josef

for Cádiz to intercept them.

The following evening, the British heard the Spanish firing signalling shots in the fog. By early the next morning, they had closed to within a few miles and, as dawn broke, the British formed up into two battle lines behind the unsuspecting Spanish. Admiral Jervis then issued his final instructions from *Victory*'s quarterdeck:

"A victory for England is essential."

It was only then that he realised the British were outnumbered two to one. It was too late to disengage, however, and he couldn't let the Spanish and French navies join forces, so he chose to form his fleet into a single line to pass between the loose Spanish columns. At 11am, Jervis gave the order for his ships to line up ahead and astern of *Victory*. Ten minutes later, he instructed his ships to engage the enemy at the Battle of Cape St Vincent.

Jervis's decision to pass between the loosely formed enemy lines was inspired: he could engage his port and starboard weaponry while the Spanish would have to limit their fire for fear of missing the British fleet and striking their own ships (solid round cannon shot frequently skipped across the water for hundreds of metres and skilled gunners even used the effect to enhance their range).

After an hour, the British fleet tacked away from the smaller Spanish column in the southeast to give chase to the larger squadron in the northwest. The Spanish lee division saw an opportunity to split the British column but, every time their ships approached, they received raking broadsides, particularly from *Victory* as

she came to the tacking point. The small Spanish cluster then tried to join up with the main force so that both could run to Cádiz. Jervis countered by signalling his fleet to take positions for mutual support and then engage the enemy in succession.

Nelson was now commanding HMS *Captain*, but he interpreted this signal rather loosely (some would argue that he disobeyed it completely and would have been court-martialled if his action had been unsuccessful). He instructed Captain Ralph Miller to remove *Captain* from the line and engage the larger Spanish group. It was a brave decision as this took the *Captain* across the bows of the biggest and most heavily armed ship in the world, the 130-gun *Santísima Trinidad*, as well as five more ships of 74-112 guns.

By the time the *Culloden* and the remaining British ships at the head of their line overhauled the Spanish rear, *Captain* had been trading fire with the six enemy ships for half an hour. As *Orion*, *Blenheim* and *Prince George* drew some of the heat away from *Captain*, she was able to make repairs and restock with shot. *Excellent*, *Diadem* and *Victory* then forced the *San Ysidro*

RIGHT The Infante don
Pelayo races in to battle
to rescue the Santisima
Trinidad

and *Salvator del Mundo* to surrender.

Captain, meanwhile, had taken such a fearful pounding that she'd lost her wheel and foretopmast and had become uncontrollable. Nelson and Miller continued firing her portside guns point blank into the Spanish fleet and her crew eventually boarded and captured the *San Nicolás* and the *San José*. It was an outrageously bold manoeuvre to use one enemy ship as a bridge to another but Nelson's gamble paid off and both enemy captains surrendered their swords to him.

Nelson secured both captured ships, then transferred his pennant from the disabled *Captain* to *Irresistible*. At the end of the battle, still wearing his ruined uniform and covered in powder and nursing two minor injuries, Nelson was summoned aboard *Victory*. Jervis received him on the quarterdeck and could have dressed him down for his insubordination but he knew when to reward bravery and initiative and couldn't praise Nelson enough. *Captain* had taken a third of all British casualties during the engagement, but she had inflicted terrible damage and casualties to the Spanish flagship and to the two captured ships. His action also resulted in 3,000 prisoners being taken.

The remaining Spanish ships escaped but the Royal Navy had shown that a smaller and more organised force could overwhelm superior numbers – in terms of both ships and men – with better seamanship, tactics and communication. Indeed, when the Spanish ships were examined, many of the guns still had their tampions (plugs) in their muzzles. Firing these cannon would have caused more damage to the ship than if they'd been struck with enemy shot.

On returning to Britain, Jervis was made Baron of Meaford and Earl St Vincent. He was also granted a life pension and the freedom of London, and he then received a gold medal from the king. He returned to sea to resume the blockade of Cádiz until hostilities ceased with the Peace of Amiens in 1802.

Nelson was knighted for his role at Cape St Vincent, and he was then promoted to rear-admiral, not for service during the battle but because he was next in line to be promoted to flag rank on seniority. He was also presented with a ceremonial sword. *Victory* underwent a major refit costing the equivalent of another £50 million and was then repainted in her black-and-yellow colour scheme. Thereafter, Nelson and *Victory* would be inextricably linked.

Horatio Nelson

Nelson was born to the Reverend Edmund and his wife Catherine on September 29, 1758 in Burnham Thorpe in Norfolk. He was the sixth of their 11 children and was named after his godfather, Horatio Walpole (his mother was grandniece of Robert Walpole, the first British Prime Minister, but she died when Nelson was only nine). Nelson was a fragile youngster and his parents feared he wouldn't survive but he grew into a robust child.

Nelson went to Palston Grammar School until he was 12 and then had a brief spell at King Edward's in Norwich. He embarked on his distinguished naval career at the same age when he reported to Captain Maurice Suckling (a maternal uncle) as an ordinary seaman aboard HMS *Raisonnable*. He was soon promoted to midshipman and began training to be an officer, although he suffered from terrible seasickness.

During peacetime, Nelson served aboard merchant ships sailing to the West Indies, and he was then coxswain on Constantine Phipps's unsuccessful mission to find the famed Northwest Passage. He first saw action in the Indian Ocean when two ships of the Sultan of Mysore attacked his ship, HMS *Seahorse*, in early 1775. He spent the rest of the year escorting convoys and honing his seamanship and navigational skills. He then contracted malaria, however, and might have died had he not been transferred home

aboard HMS *Dolphin*.

He had recovered sufficiently by the time he arrived back in London that he was promoted to acting lieutenant aboard HMS *Worcester*, an escort to the Gibraltar convoys. He passed his lieutenant's exams in 1777 and was dispatched to HMS *Lowestoffe* under Captain William Locker. The ship captured several enemy vessels during the American War of Independence and Nelson was given command of the tender *Little Lucy*. He was developing into such a fine seaman that Locker recommended him to Sir Peter Parker, commander-in-chief of Jamaica. Parker recruited Nelson to his flagship, HMS *Bristol*, and the two captured many more enemy ships in 1778. He then promoted Nelson to commander of the brig HMS *Badger*.

Nelson cruised the Gulf of Mexico for most of the following year before being promoted to post-captain of the captured French 28-gun frigate *Astrée*. It was promptly renamed HMS *Hinchinbrook* but Nelson had barely taken command when he was sent to Fort Charles on Jamaica to protect it against the incoming French fleet. The French veered north and the invasion never

materialised so Nelson accompanied Major-General John Dalling's attack on the Spanish colonies on the mainland. Nelson secured the surrender of Castillo Viejo in Costa Rica but he decided to destroy the fort and retreat when his men were decimated by disease. Having returned to Jamaica, he was given command of the 44-gun frigate HMS *Janus*, but Nelson was still suffering the after-effects of malaria and was invalided back to Britain. He eventually recovered but it wasn't until late 1781 that he took command of his next ship, HMS *Albermarle*.

He spent the next two years escorting convoys in North America and capturing small enemy ships along the eastern seaboard and throughout the Caribbean. The 1783 Treaty of Paris brought peace so Nelson returned to England. He contemplated a move into politics but was then tasked with enforcing the Navigation Acts (a series of laws governing trade between Britain and the colonies) around Antigua. During his placement in the West Indies, he met and married Frances Nisbet, widow of one of the plantation owners, at the Montpelier Estate on Nevis in 1787.

Nelson and his wife returned to Brit-

ain and divided their time between Bath, London and his childhood home in Norfolk. He lobbied to be given another command but Britain's relationship with the French and Spanish had warmed and there were no ships available. When the French annexed Belgium in 1792, Nelson was recalled to the navy. The following January he assumed command of HMS *Agamemnon* and headed to Gibraltar to help Britain establish control of the Mediterranean. When the city of Toulon asked for his protection from the French National Convention, Nelson sailed to Sardinia and Naples to drum up reinforcements.

In Naples he was introduced to William Hamilton, the British Ambassador, and his wife, Emma. Nelson returned to Toulon with 2,000 men in October but the French were already bombarding the city so Nelson sailed to Cagliari and Tunis to drum up more support. He was then given command of a small squadron to blockade the French on Corsica. Toulon eventually fell so Nelson was dispatched to establish a base on Corsica as a consolation.

He directed the bombardment of enemy positions at Calvi in June 1794 and then oversaw the troop landings and gun deployments around the town. On July 12, some shot struck one of the sandbags surrounding his position and debris sprayed into Nelson's right eye. He was immediately patched up and returned to the frontline, however. The following week, Nelson and his men stormed and captured the main defensive positions. He then bombarded the town into submission by early August. It was clear that the damage to his eye was permanent, however, and he eventually lost the use of it.

He refused to let the injury affect his career and put to sea in the spring of 1795 to counter the threat of a French attack on Corsica. The two fleets shadowed each other in early March, although Nelson engaged the enemy at every opportunity and eventually captured the *Ça Ira* and the *Censeur*. He fought several small skirmishes throughout the summer but, with little action to keep him busy, he devised plans for amphibious landings and revised outdated naval tactics. He was unable to convince Admiral William Hotham or his successor, Sir Hyde Parker, of their importance and the French eventually forced the British out of Italy. Nelson was disheartened

LEFT Frances 'Fanny' Nisbet became Nelson's first wife in 1787

HORATIO NELSON

RIGHT HMS Agamemnon (left) trades broadsides with the Ca Ira in 1795

FAR RIGHT Nelson secures the surrender of the San Nicolas at the Battle of Cape St Vincent

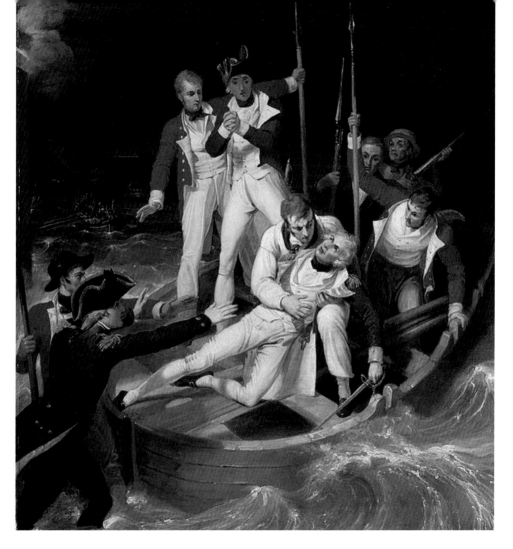

by their lack of ambition and contemplated retirement.

Command of the Mediterranean Fleet then passed to Sir John Jervis. He promoted Nelson to commodore and appointed him to HMS *Captain* when *Agamemnon* was sent home for repairs. When the French attacked and took the port city of Livorno in northwest Italy, Nelson oversaw the evacuation of the British presence and then blockaded the harbour. But continual French pressure with Genoese assistance forced the British to abandon their pretensions in the Mediterranean and retreat to Gibraltar.

Having captured the Spanish frigate *Santa Sabina*, and then escaped from a much larger fleet, Nelson rescued captured British crews in Cartagena before rendezvousing with Jervis off Cádiz. The enemy fleets then met at the Battle of Cape St Vincent, where Nelson's incredible capture of two Spanish warships overshadowed his disregard for orders.

He took command of a new flagship, HMS *Theseus*, and then bombarded Cádiz. He led the subsequent amphibious landing, although he was almost killed on two occasions when the fighting became hand-to-hand on a barge in the harbour. Seaman John Sykes sustained serious injuries in the battle but saved Nelson on both occasions.

Nelson used similar tactics when trying to capture Santa Cruz de Tenerife, but the Spanish were alerted after the first landing attempt failed in poor weather. This gave them time to regroup and they repelled two further naval bombardments and beach assaults. Nelson's landing party was one of the only boats to come ashore at the right point but he was then struck in the right elbow by musket fire. The ball shattered his humerus so he was evacuated to the *Theseus*.

Nelson insisted that Doctor Thomas Eshelby amputate most of the arm and he was back on duty within an hour. He had to oversee a negotiated withdrawal, however. British land forces under Sir Thomas Troubridge had fought their way into the town but their boats had been sunk so no reinforcements could land. The Spanish commander allowed them to retreat but a quarter of the landing party were already dead.

Nelson took responsibility for the failure and went back to England aboard HMS *Seahorse* with the intention of standing down. He returned to

LEFT Nelson lies wounded during the Battle for Santa Cruz on Tenerife

a hero's welcome, however. News had spread of his courage during the Battle of Cape St Vincent and his wounds only garnered him sympathy. His failure to capture Santa Cruz was overlooked completely.

He spent time recovering from his injuries but he was keen to be given another command. He was eventually assigned to HMS *Vanguard* and ordered to monitor French fleet movements off Toulon. Nelson soon learned that Napoleon was attacking Malta but he arrived too late to prevent the island surrendering. He then chased the French across the Mediterranean until he finally cornered the enemy fleet at Aboukir Bay near Alexandria on the Nile estuary.

The French outnumbered the British and they were in a strong position close to a line of shoals, which would force the British to attack the bigger ships to the rear of their line. As it was late, Vice-Admiral François-Paul Brueys d'Aigalliers thought Nelson would wait until first light to attack but Nelson immediately manoeuvred his fleet close to the shore and instructed Captain Thomas Foley on HMS *Goliath* to navigate between the French fleet and the shoals so they could attack from both sides.

Half the British fleet followed Foley down the port side, while the rest pummelled the starboard line. Brueys didn't believe the shoals were navigable so he hadn't prepared his portside weapons and the entire French fleet was soon caught in a withering crossfire. Brueys had also forgotten to close up the gaps so several British ships penetrated the line and pounded the French into submission. To make matters worse, Napoleon hadn't resupplied the French and hundreds of men who had been sent ashore to buy provisions were now under attack from Bedouin tribesmen.

Nelson was directing the battle from *Vanguard*'s quarterdeck as she engaged first *Spartiate* and then *Aquilon*. He was then struck in the forehead by a splinter of shot, which caused a flap of skin to cover his good eye. Nelson was convinced he would die but the surgeon soon patched up the wound and he was back on deck in time to see the French flagship *L'Orient* catch fire and explode.

The battle was of such strategic importance – it halted Napoleon's advance in the eastern Mediterranean

– that many historians rate the victory as the most significant in Nelson's career. Two French ships were destroyed and nine more were captured, and Napoleon's stranded ground forces were then defeated at the Siege of Acre.

Nelson oversaw the repairs to his fleet before sailing for Naples. He was again hosted by the Hamiltons and his affection for Emma didn't go unnoticed. He was also honoured with banquets and balls, and he even began attending with Emma at his side. He was then tasked with retaking Rome from the French. The Neapolitan army under General Mack surrounded the city in November 1798 but, although they briefly moved into the city, a French counterattack forced them all the way back to Naples.

Nelson was on hand to organise the evacuation over Christmas and the French finally took the city in January. Nelson blockaded the port and supported Cardinal Ruffo's attempt to recapture Naples in the spring. Ruffo forced the French to retreat but his troops were ill disciplined and society collapsed. Nelson insisted that the rebels should surrender unconditionally, although he then tried and executed the majority.

He was promoted to the senior officer in the Mediterranean theatre but he didn't put to sea again until 1800. Nelson immediately captured a French ship but he was still refusing to take orders and his relationship with Emma Hamilton was becoming embarrassing. Nelson might have ignored their pleas for him to return to England but the Hamiltons eventually decided to head back so the decision was taken for him. Nelson wanted to return by sea but the Hamiltons chose to travel overland via Trieste, Vienna, Prague, Dresden and Hamburg before catching a ship to Great Yarmouth.

Nelson arrived home to another hero's welcome but his marriage broke down immediately when he swore allegiance to Emma. She bore him a daughter, Horatia, in January 1801, but Nelson was back on active duty within weeks: British ships blockading French ports had imposed a right to stop and search vessels from Russia, Prussia, Denmark and Sweden. These governments had grown tired of the intrusion and decided to ignore the British navy as they were interfering with legitimate trade.

Admiral Sir Hyde Parker's fleet sailed for Denmark in March 1801.

Parker wanted to block the entrance to the Baltic but Nelson suggested attacking the Danish fleet at anchor in Copenhagen. Parker reluctantly agreed, although it initially appeared to be the wrong decision as three British ships ran aground. The Danish shore batteries then opened up and caused significant casualties. Parker raised a signal suggesting Nelson withdraw but, somewhat typically, Nelson put his telescope to his bad eye and ignored it: "I have only one eye so I have a right to be blind sometimes. I really do not see the signal. Damn the signal. Keep mine for close action flying."

After three hours of intense fighting, both fleets were in disarray and Nelson asked Crown Prince Frederick to concede to a truce, to which the Danish commander agreed. An armistice was signed and Nelson was made Commander of the Baltic and Viscount of the Nile when he returned to England.

Nelson was then tasked with patrolling the French coast to warn of an invasion by Napoleon, but an uneasy peace (Amiens: 1801) and poor health saw him recalled to London. He spent the next three years touring the country before settling down at Merton Place in Surrey. In May 1803, war again broke out with France. Nelson was assigned to HMS *Victory* as Commander of the Mediterranean Fleet.

Napoleon Bonaparte was determined to halt a succession of French defeats to the English and even drew up plans to invade the islands, but the main obstacle was the navy patrolling the English Channel. Napoleon's immediate problem was that his own navy was blockaded in ports from Brest to Toulon, but he still raised an army of 120,000 in the Pas de Calais. He knew he only had to control the straits for a few hours and his army could be dropped on England's south coast. Napoleon may have been a brilliant tactician and ground commander but he was inexperienced on water. His plan was to send Admiral Villeneuve out into the Atlantic so that Nelson would be forced into a pursuit. With *Victory* and the main fleet occupied, the English Channel would be poorly protected and Napoleon could make his move.

The course of naval history was about to change forever.

The Battle of Trafalgar

Nelson joined *Victory* in Portsmouth and immediately sailed for Malta to meet up with the rest of his squadron. As admiral of the fleet, he played little part in the day-to-day running of the ship, however. This was down to Captain Thomas Hardy and his crew of lieutenants, junior officers and midshipmen.

The officers were professional sailors but half of the ship's company of 850 men were volunteers, notably the highly skilled marines (who maintained discipline aboard ship) and younger boys learning their trade to become ordinary or able seamen. In peacetime, crews were limited but conscription was often necessary in times of conflict. Despite rumours of terrible conditions and food, life in the navy was often easier than on land. Nelson was particularly conscientious and regularly dispatched boats to the mainland to collect fresh water and provisions so his crew could eat three meals a day.

He blockaded Toulon for 18 months but then retreated to form a looser line around the port in the hope that this would draw the French out into battle. However, a storm in January 1805 then scattered the British ships so Admiral Pierre-Charles Villeneuve's fleet ran the blockade. Nelson gave chase throughout the eastern Mediterranean only to learn that poor weather had forced Villeneuve back into Toulon. The French fleet again gave Nelson the slip and Villeneuve escaped through the Strait of

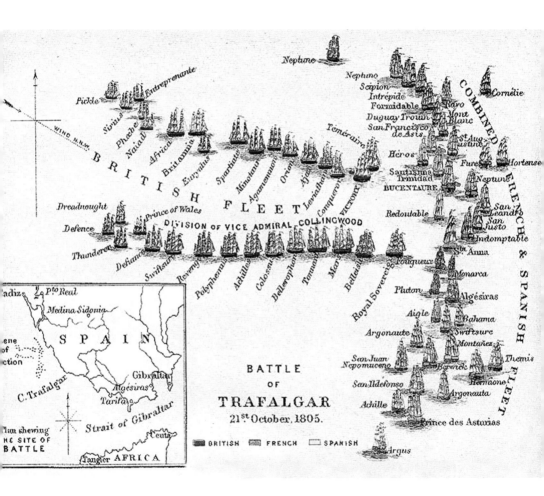

BATTLE
OF
TRAFALGAR
21st October, 1805.

BRITISH FRENCH SPANISH

Gibraltar to the West Indies.

Nelson didn't want the incident blighting his service record so he took up the chase. He spent the whole of June searching the Caribbean without realising that Villeneuve had ignored Napoleon's orders and doubled back to Europe. With Nelson racing back east, Captain Robert Calder finally intercepted the French off Cape Finisterre. The engagement itself was indecisive and Villeneuve escaped to Ferrol on the north coast of Spain. Despite securing a strategic victory, Calder was severely reprimanded for not pursuing the enemy fleet and

he never served at sea again.

A frustrated and despondent Nelson expected similar treatment for his failure to contain the French but he was lionised on his return to Britain for preventing a French invasion of British colonies in the West Indies. He became more determined than ever to safeguard his legacy so he drew up plans to annihilate the enemy fleet when he next saw action.

Nelson was presented with a chance when Captain Henry Blackwood arrived at Merton Place to let him know that the entire French and Spanish fleets were at anchor in Cádiz. Nelson headed to London to discuss his plans with Lord Castlereagh, during which he briefly met Major-General Arthur

Wellesley (the future Duke of Wellington). Wellesley was initially unimpressed with Nelson, believing him self-centred and shallow but, when Nelson realised who Wellesley was, he engaged him in conversation about the war, life in the colonies and world politics and made something of an impression on the young commander. Nelson then headed back to Portsmouth to meet up with *Victory*. He was feted as a national hero wherever he went and many onlookers knelt before him as he climbed aboard ship.

Victory reached Cádiz in late September and Nelson assumed command of the fleet from Rear-Admiral Collingwood. With the French trapped in the port, Nelson took the opportunity to

BELOW Nelson's penultimate signal before the battle

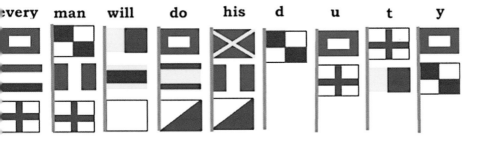

every   man   will   do   his   d   u   t   y

brief his captains on his plan, which had been modified having learned the lessons from the Nile, Copenhagen and Camperdown engagements: instead of forming up opposite the French in a single parallel line, he would split the British fleet into two columns that would pierce the French line at right-angles and divide it into thirds. Although the centre of the French fleet could unleash their entire portside weapons in the initial stages, their front and rear squadrons wouldn't be able to engage at all (they'd be out of range), and the British would be able to fire with both sides once the French column had been penetrated. This should allow the British to destroy the middle of the French line before the van and rear squadron could come to the rescue. It was an inspired tactic that would become known as crossing the T. (In the hours before the battle, Nelson drew his battle line on the map in wine from his glass.)

Napoleon, meanwhile, was expecting his fleet to break out of Cádiz and meet up with reinforcements from the Mediterranean in Brest on the northwest coast of France. His combined fleet would then clear the English Channel and provide cover from the remnants of the Royal Navy as his invasion barges delivered troops for the conquest of Britain. It was the plan he'd been waiting two years to implement but he'd not taken the chance when Nelson was pursuing Villeneuve across the Atlantic as the Royal Navy's presence in the channel was still overwhelming. Napoleon was becoming impatient, however, and he had to strike before the winter storms.

Admiral William Cornwallis saw an opportunity to catch the French out and dispatched Vice-Admiral Calder with 20 ships from the Channel Fleet to join Nelson off Cádiz. This left only a dozen ships blockading Brest and defending the south coast of England but Napoleon wasn't ready to invade and the gamble paid off. Calder and Nelson's combined fleet then gathered off Cádiz at the end of September.

Nelson again tried to lure the Franco-Spanish fleet out by dispatching smaller frigates to patrol the harbour but they didn't take the bait. Nelson then lost Calder and his flagship *Prince of Wales* when the captain was summoned home for his court-martial over the Finisterre incident. He also lost five ships-of-the-line to convoy duty in the Mediterranean. However, several more ships arrived in the first weeks of October to resupply his fleet. By the middle of the month, Nelson was ready. And he talked only of annihilating the allied Franco-Spanish fleet.

Villeneuve, on the other hand, was not. His return run across the Atlantic had used up vital supplies, and a prolonged stay in Cádiz had seen his crews neglect gunnery practice. Many were inexperienced at sea, particularly in battle, and their overland supply lines were not delivering enough provisions or ammunition. Despite receiving orders from Napoleon to put to sea as soon as possible, Villeneuve asked his captains for their opinion and, when they learned of Nelson's arrival, they voted overwhelmingly to remain in port. The French were also sandbagged by events during the 'terror' as many outstanding naval officers had been executed in the revolution, further weakening their military. Without these expert navigators, seafarers and commanders, they were in no condition to fight the British. Indeed, their ships were often crewed by prematurely promoted midshipmen, militarily inex-

perienced merchant-ship captains and civilian volunteers.

On October 18, however, Villeneuve suddenly gave the order to leave port in light winds. Word had come though that Vice-Admiral François Rosily was about to replace him as Master of the Combined Fleet so, rather than endure the disgrace of being relieved of command, he put to sea. The fleet formed up slowly and loosely and it wasn't until two days later that they began heading southeast for Gibraltar.

Despite having lost the six ships of Admiral Loius' squadron to Gibraltar earlier in the month, Nelson immediately gave chase to the superior Franco-Spanish fleet and his ships thundered south with the wind behind them. Villeneuve could see them closing and ordered his ships into three columns to negate any chance the British had of penetrating their lines. He then changed his mind and signalled for them to return to single file but the message was confusing and his fleet was soon somewhat scattered.

On the morning of October 21, as the *Victory* neared Cape Trafalgar some 40 miles west of Gibraltar, Nelson gave the order to prepare for battle. He then fin-

THE BATTLE OF TRAFALGAR

RIGHT Admiral
Cuthbert Collingwood
led the southern line of
attack on HMS Royal
Sovereign

ished up some paperwork and noted in his journal that he wanted the government to give Emma Hamilton ample provision to maintain her rank in life and ensure she could raise her daughter. He also wrote a short prayer while at the breakfast table in the day cabin, which doubled as his office.

At 8am, Villeneuve decided to try running for Cádiz and ordered his fleet about, but the winds were light and it took nearly two hours for his inexperienced seamen to complete the manoeuvre. His fleet was now spread north to south in a slight parabola. Nelson realised Villeneuve's line was broken and confused so he ordered his ships into two columns and prepared to split the enemy into three with the flagship stranded in the middle.

As *Victory* approached the French line, a Royal Marine drummer sounded a 'Beat to Quarters' roll (the equivalent of 'Action Stations!' today). Then Captain Thomas Hardy ordered the decks cleared for action to reduce the danger from flying splinters. This meant storing all mess tables, benches, sea chests and other furniture below. His well-drilled crew removed all the surplus equipment in 10 minutes. The crew

then manned their cannon for the engagement. (It may come as a surprise that only around two thirds of *Victory*'s crew were British. There were also 22 Americans fighting alongside smaller numbers from Sweden, Holland, Italy, the West Indies and even France. Records suggest that a Jane Townsend was also among the crews at Trafalgar.)

Nelson was outnumbered (approximately 30,000 enemy sailors to his 17,000) and outgunned (33 ships-of-the-line with 2,568 guns to his 27 and 2,148) but his tactics held the key. Conventional wisdom had the fleets line up opposite one another and keep firing until one side capitulated after the resulting mêlée. It was easier to signal ships in line so a commander retained control over his fleet for longer. Ships that were damaged could also withdraw without endangering their own fleet. These tactics led to indecisive results, however, and Nelson wanted outright victory.

His method would isolate the enemy flagship (and its squadron) in the centre of the opposing fleet so that it could be surrounded and destroyed. Shot fired longitudinally through the poorly protected bow and stern of the enemy

fleet would also kill many more men as the cannonballs could travel the length of each ship. Whereas a single broadside might kill the six men at one position, a longitudinal shot could account for up to 40 men. Help from the front and rear squadrons would be difficult to organise with the loss of signalling from the flagship, and it would take time for subordinate captains to assume control of the situation.

Crossing the T relied on heading for the enemy at full speed to minimise the time the front squadron would be subjected to the raking Franco-Spanish broadsides. It also prevented enemy ships escaping from the engagement. It would then allow a general mêlée to develop, in which the highly trained British seamen and marines would have the advantage (their skill, morale and gunnery were far superior to the demoralised enemy). If all else failed, Nelson instructed his captains to run alongside the enemy ships and blast them at close quarters. He had also insisted his ships were repainted with a yellow-and-black chequer so that they were distinguishable from the Franco-Spanish fleet.

Nelson may have been outnumbered but his men were supremely confident, even if they knew the fate of England depended on the outcome of a single naval battle. Just before midday, Nelson joined Signal Officer John Pasco on the poop of the *Victory* and asked him to send the message: 'England confides that every man will do his duty.' Pasco knew that the word 'confides' wasn't in the signal book and would have to be spelt out so he suggested substituting it for 'expects', which only used one flag. Nelson agreed to the change and then ordered 'Engage the enemy more closely' to be sent. This order remained in place until it was destroyed during the battle. The fact that Nelson had taken the time to compose the messages and then ensure his ships received them gave his men a tremendous boost. Admiral Collingwood, who was spearheading the second line of attack in HMS *Royal Sovereign*, was less than impressed, however, apparently muttering: "What is Nelson signalling about? We all know what we have to do." It's not surprising that his response hasn't aged as well as Nelson's signal.

Captain Thomas Hardy suggested that HMS *Temeraire* should spearhead the northern attack line in case *Victory*

THE BATTLE OF TRAFALGAR

was damaged in the initial thrust. Nelson overruled him and also declined to take a backseat aboard the frigate HMS *Euryalus* because he wanted to be seen on the frontline.

Nelson then led the battle line directly at the Franco-Spanish fleet. Villeneuve was concerned that his rear squadron might become isolated but there was no time to allow them to form up so he gave the order to fire on the British at noon. The winds were still light so *Victory* was pounded for an hour before she could even bring her guns to bear. It seemed as if the weather had removed one of Nelson's advantages. Indeed, the fire was so severe that Hardy suggested Nelson remove the decorations from his jacket so he wouldn't be singled out by enemy sharpshooters as the fleets converged. Nelson again declined, insisting he was proud to show his military orders to the enemy. His secretary, John Scott, was then almost cut in two by a cannonball. Hardy's clerk took up a position at Nelson's side but he too was killed immediately along with eight marines. Nelson refused to take cover and continued barking orders to his men, but the fighting was so ferocious that he must have feared for his fleet.

Collingwood on the *Royal Sovereign* was heading for the southern end of the French line when she too came under intense bombardment from the *Fougueux*, *Indomptable*, *San Justo* and *San Leandro*. He still managed to break through the line astern of the flagship *Santa Ana* and then *Royal Sovereign* at last opened up, delivering a withering broadside into the unprotected enemy fleet. Several British ships were disabled on their approach but most poured into the breach.

To the north, *Victory*'s guns had been silent for an hour and she had been taking terrible punishment. Her wheel was destroyed so she could only be steered from the tiller below deck but she managed to pierce the enemy line between Villeneuve's flagship *Bucentaure* and the *Redoutable*. She then loosed a tremendous volley that wiped out men and equipment on the French decks. During the mêlée that followed, *Victory* and *Redoutable* collided and their rigging became entangled so the French infantry corps prepared to board.

It was then that a sniper on the *Redoutable*'s mizzentop (a small platform on the upper end of the lower mast)

LEFT HMS Victory
at Trafalgar

RIGHT Captain
Thomas Hardy

fired his musket at Nelson from a range of no more than 50 feet (15 metres). The shot struck Nelson in his left shoulder before passing through his spine and lodging just below his right shoulder blade. Nelson crumpled to the deck proclaiming that he must be dead as his spine had been shot through. Signal Midshipman John Pollard and Midshipman Francis Collingwood returned fire, with Pollard's shot killing the sniper whose identity has never been established.

Hardy instructed Sergeant-Major Robert Adair and two seamen to carry Nelson down to the orlop deck but he was still issuing orders. His crew then made him comfortable with lemonade and wine while Hardy returned topside to continue directing the battle. *Victory* was still in danger of being boarded (wooden hulls made these ships so buoyant that they rarely sank and had to be captured by boarding parties armed with pikes, cutlasses and pistols) so Hardy summoned up the gunners to repel the enemy marines. They were decimated by French grenades, however, and it took swift action from HMS *Temeraire* to save the flagship. She came alongside the *Red-*

outable and fired on the French ship with a devastating point-blank volley of 68-pound carronade shot. By 2pm, the *Redoutable*'s crew had been reduced to 100 from 750 so Captain Jean-Jacques Lucas surrendered.

HMS *Neptune*, *Leviathan* and *Conqueror* then joined the fray and between them they overwhelmed the *Bucentaure* and *Santísima Trinidad*. Four ships of the redundant allied van initially doubled back as if to attack the British but Rear-Admiral Le Pelley couldn't break through the enemy lines and chose to retreat instead. (He ran for Toulon but then changed his mind and headed for Rochefort, but he eventually ran into Sir Richard Strachan's squadron and all four ships were captured by the British at the Battle of Cape Ortegal in November.)

At half past two, Hardy headed below to check on Nelson. He informed his commander that several allied ships had already surrendered and that the battle would be won. Nelson reminded Hardy that there was a storm on the way and warned him to be at anchor by nightfall. He also asked that Emma Hamilton be looked after. He then mumbled that he could feel blood

LEFT Nelson lies
mortally wounded
on the Victory's
quarterdeck having
been shot by a
French sniper on
the Redoutable

THE BATTLE OF TRAFALGAR

RIGHT Nelson's
final moments

gushing throughout his chest so he knew he didn't have long left. He also remarked that he had no feeling in the lower part of his body and that his breathing was becoming more difficult.

Nelson insisted on being updated with the state of the battle, however. Every time an enemy ship surrendered, his crew let out an almighty roar. Nelson was concerned that *Victory* might still be boarded but Hardy comforted him that it was only the French ships that were striking their flags. When told he would be able to deliver news of the decisive victory to the monarch, Nelson knew they were only trying to keep his spirits up: "It is nonsense to suppose I can live. My sufferings are great but they will soon be over."

There is some debate over Nelson's last words but those present insisted he asked to be kept cool and hydrated. He also asked Hardy to kiss him, although by then he was delirious and barely noticed when the captain kissed him on the cheek and forehead. Surgeon Sir William Beatty saved countless lives on the *Victory* but he knew Nelson's injury couldn't be treated. He later wrote a definitive account of the battle and insisted Nelson murmured "Thank God I

have done my duty." The chaplain, Alexander Scott, said that when Nelson's pulse was taken for the final time a few moments later, he muttered "God and my country." He died at 4.30pm, three hours after being shot.

The loss of their commanding officer affected the British deeply and was perhaps best summed up by Captain Henry Blackwood: "In my life, I was never so shocked or completely upset as upon me flying to the *Victory*, even before the action was over, to find Lord Nelson was then at the gasp of death. Such an admiral has the country lost, and every officer and man so kind, so good, so obliging a friend as never was." Collingwood's men on the *Royal Sovereign* had fought like the possessed but they were now reduced to tears as the terrible news filtered through.

The battle was won over the next hour but the cost had been extremely high on both sides: the British had lost 450 men and another 1,300 had been wounded, but they had not lost a single ship and the Franco-Spanish losses were far worse. One ship was completely destroyed, another 21 were captured, 3,000 men were killed in the battle and a similar number perished

in the storm afterwards, and another 10,000 were captured or wounded. It was perhaps the most decisive naval victory in military history.

The storm immediately afterwards scuppered Collingwood's plans to tow the captured ships to port and he only managed to save four. The *Redoutable* and *Bucentaure* were abandoned and eventually sank so his prize money was a fraction of what it could have been.

The Franco-Spanish losses were so severe, and building replacement ships was so time-consuming and costly, that they couldn't threaten the British navy for the remainder of the Napoleonic Wars. Indeed, the Royal Navy wasn't engaged in a fleet-to-fleet battle until Jutland in the First World War more than a century later. Trafalgar's legacy is therefore one of undisputed naval supremacy throughout the world's oceans. This boosted Britain's international trade, which made the country so rich and powerful that its empire soon spanned a quarter of the globe.

HMS *Victory* was badly damaged during the intense bombardment in the first hour of the battle and had to be towed to Gibraltar by HMS *Neptune*.

(More than 90 cannonballs and other projectiles punctured her foretopsail.) She also bore the brunt of the casualties with 57 men killed and 110 injured.

Midshipman R Roberts provided a more comprehensive account of the damage sustained by *Victory* in the ship's remark book: 'The hull is shot through in a number of places, including several along the waterline. More beams and riders have their knees shot through, and there's a broken starboard cathead. Timbers of the head and stem are full of shot with most parts damaged. Chains and channels have been shot away and the mizzenmast has also been shot away nine feet above the deck. The bulwarks are shot away, the mainmast is full of shot and sprung, the main yard has gone, and the main topmast cap has been shot away. The main topsail mast yard has been destroyed. The foremast is shot through in many places, the foreyard is shot away along with the bowsprit, jib boom and cap. The sprit-sail yards and flying-jib boom are gone. The fore and main tops have been shot away and the ship is taking on 12 inches of water an hour.'

Nelson's body was stored in a brandy cask and covered in camphor (a flammable waxy substance found in the wood of the camphor laurel that was used for embalming) and myrrh (an aromatic resin). The cask was then tied to *Victory*'s mainmast and placed under armed guard for the voyage to Gibraltar.

When the ship reached the rock on October 28, Nelson's body was transferred to a lead-lined coffin that was filled with aqua vitae (distilled wine). Having undergone repairs to her masts and rigging, *Victory* then transported Nelson's body back to Britain, although poor weather meant she didn't arrive until December 5. When news reached London of his death, Lady Hamilton was inconsolable and couldn't speak for 10 hours. Even King George III was reduced to tears: "We have lost more than we gained."

Victory docked at the Nore Sandbank at the mouth of the Thames Estuary and unloaded Nelson's body onto dockyard commissioner Sir George Grey's yacht *Chatham* for the trip upriver to Greenwich. He was then placed in another lead coffin that was surrounded by a wooden casket made from the mast of *L'Orient*, the enemy flagship having been salvaged after being destroyed at the Battle of the Nile.

Nelson lay in state in the Painted Hall at Greenwich for three days before he was loaded aboard a funeral barge and taken to the admiralty for the night. The following morning, his funeral procession left the admiralty accompanied by 32 admirals, more than 100 captains and 10,000 soldiers. The service on January 9, 1806 took place at St Paul's Cathedral and was attended by George III (who would have been chief mourner had royal protocol not intervened), Sir Peter Parker, seven dukes and 16 earls. After the service, Nelson was laid to rest in a sarcophagus that had been carved for Cardinal Wolsey. His body was placed directly beneath the dome in the centre of the cathedral.

Nelson remained a focal figure for the British in times of crisis, war and social upheaval. Monuments were immediately raised to him – specifically Nelson's Column in Trafalgar Square – and he is said to have inspired Churchill during the darkest days of the Second World War. Such was his influence that he was voted the ninth Greatest Briton in history in a BBC poll in 2002.

Chapter 5

Life after Trafalgar

RIGHT HMS Victory's
Trafalgar colour
scheme

Having been repaired in the dock-yard at Chatham (where her keel had been laid half a century earlier), Victory immediately re-entered service. Her wheel had been destroyed at Trafalgar so the new one bore the inscription of Nelson's 'England expects' signal and a plaque had been attached to the quarterdeck where he'd been struck down.

Admiral James Saumarez assumed command and headed for the Baltic to blockade ports under French control in northern Germany. This enraged the Russians and Swedes and Alexander I re-opened Russian ports in 1810. The French then convinced Sweden to declare war on the British but Saumarez was primarily a peacemaker and he cor-

rectly predicted that both the Russians and Swedes would turn on Napoleon. Denmark was then part of the French Empire so Saumarez monitored shipping around Copenhagen until the Swedes invaded in 1814.

By then, *Victory* had been taken out of service and she was eventually moored close to the harbour entrance in Portsmouth in November 1812. The final entry in her log reads: *Moderate breezes and snowy weather. Ship returning the remaining stores to the victualling office and dockyard. P.H. Dumaresq. Captain.*

She was initially used as a depot ship but gradually fell into disrepair as steam propulsion made sails obsolete. By 1831, the Industrial Revolution had gripped the country and she was little more than a rotting hulk. Thomas

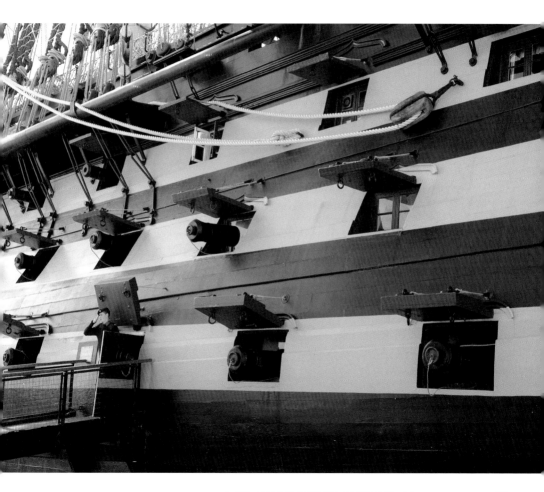

Hardy, now the first sea lord, signed an order for the ship to be broken up. Although the story may be apocryphal (the page in the duty log went missing immediately thereafter), Hardy's wife, Anna Louisa Berkeley, apparently begged him to reconsider. Hardy eventually rescinded the order but no maintenance work was scheduled and the ship was barely afloat when visited by the Duchess of Kent and her daughter, the future Queen Victoria, in 1833.

Another half century would pass before a use was found for the ship: in 1889 she was converted into the navy's school of telegraphy and she soon became a finishing school for officers and enlisted men learning signals on two-month training courses. With the first centenary of Trafalgar looming, the navy decided that the ship should fly Nelson's famous 'England expects' signal from her mizzenmast every October 21. (The original signal book was only introduced to the navy by Rear-Admiral Sir Home Popham four years before Trafalgar.)

In 1903, HMS *Neptune* was being towed to the breakers when she slipped her lines and struck the *Victory*, holing her below the waterline and almost sinking her. It took King Edward VII to intervene to stop her being scrapped but she was too badly damaged to maintain the signal school. It was transferred to HMS *Hercules* the following year before it took up its permanent home in the naval barracks at Chatham.

The centenary of Trafalgar brought about renewed public interest in the ship and she was decorated with electric lights powered by a submarine moored alongside. Five years later, the Society for Nautical Research was tasked with saving *Victory* but the admiralty withdrew funding as the country geared up for war once more. By 1911, Frank Mason described *Victory*'s condition as 'nothing short of an insult' in his list of British ships.

It wasn't until three years after the Great War that shipping magnate Sir James Caird launched a Save the *Victory* campaign with an initial donation of £50,000 and then another contribution of £15,000. (Caird is not to be confused with philanthropist James Key Caird who sponsored Ernest Shackleton's ill-fated trip to the Antarctic in 1914.)

In January 1922, *Victory* was finally moved into Portsmouth's Number 2 drydock (the oldest still in use) so that

BELOW The Victory is moved to the drydock for repairs in 1922

RIGHT Restoring the
Victory in 1925

the repair work restoring her to the Battle of Trafalgar configuration could be completed. Her bow was found to have dropped by 18 inches and her stern by eight inches due to a warping of her keel. The first phase of the operation took seven years and reinforced the ship's structure from the waterline to the middeck and up. This involved replacing much of the hull and reconstructing all three decks. Despite King George V unveiling a plaque commemorating the completion of the work in 1928, the Society for Nautical Research continued working on the hull into the 1930s.

The project was temporarily abandoned during the Second World War. In March 1941, a 500-pound German

bomb destroyed one of the support cradles and part of the foremast. The Nazis pounced on a propaganda opportunity to dent British morale and the admiralty was forced to issue a denial that the ship had been completely destroyed.

Several bulkheads were removed in the 1950s so that the ship could be fumigated against the deathwatch beetle, and many of the older oak hull timbers were then replaced with oily tropical hardwoods like teak, iroko and mahogany that were also resistant to fungi. The majority of the restoration was finally finished in time for the 200th anniversary of the Battle of Trafalgar in 2005, although another £16 million contract was awarded to BAE Systems in 2011 in the hope that they would complete work on the masts, rigging, side planking and fire-control systems.

It is a sad inevitability that little of the original ship was left after the recent restoration. Indeed, the largest single artefact that survives from Trafalgar is the 54-foot by 80-foot foretopsail, although it's in a poor state of repair. The sail covers more than 3,000 square feet and weighs nearly half a ton, and it took 1,200 man-hours to stitch. Although 90% of the lower gun deck is also original, only 75% of the orlop deck remains, and perhaps as little as 20% of the upper decks, masts and rigging. Part of the stern and some of the keel are still original timbers, however.

The following year, ownership of the *Victory* transferred from the Ministry of Defence to a dedicated trust within the National Museum of the Royal Navy. The Gosling Foundation and MOD then donated £50 million to the trust so that it had a budget to preserve the *Victory* for the next five years.

Victory now rests on reinforced cradles so that tourists can see the hull below the original waterline. The ship can be hired out for functions for up to 260 people, with the Great Cabin accommodating 20 guests who can experience the surroundings Nelson lived and worked in more than two centuries ago.

The ship is part of the National Historic Fleet and is listed as the flagship of the first sea lord. As such, she is the oldest commissioned warship in the world. In September 2011, Lieutenant-Commander Rod Stathern became her 100th commanding officer. Throughout her 250-year story, many of *Victory*'s masters have left their mark on maritime history.

Chapter 6

Notable Admirals and Captains of HMS Victory

CAPTAIN JOHN LINDSAY

RIGHT A young
Sir John Lindsay

Lindsay was born into a privileged family in Dornoch in Scotland in 1737. He was privately educated and joined the navy as a teenager during the Seven Years' War. He was promoted to lieutenant in 1756 and attacked Rochefort with Sir Edward Hawke the following year. He was then appointed captain of the frigate HMS *Trent*, a position he held for the next six years, during which he served with the Channel Fleet as well as capturing several Spanish ships in the West Indies.

He inherited command of the 80-gun ship-of-the-line HMS *Cambridge* when Captain William Goostrey was killed by a sniper on the *Morro Castle* but, despite being offered this and other ships on a permanent basis, he returned to the *Trent* and was knighted on his homecoming in 1764. He then successfully ran for Parliament and served as the MP for Aberdeen Burghs.

Having been promoted to commodore at the age of just 32, Lindsay took command of the *Stag* and ran the East Indies Station. He was recalled to England after uncovering illegal dealings between the East India Company and the local nawabs, however. He was then named as the first captain of HMS *Victory* but his tenure in the great ship was short-lived: when Admiral Augustus Keppel raised his flag on *Victory*, he chose John Campbell as his flag captain instead.

Lindsay took command of the *Prince George* but was then embroiled in the controversy surrounding the First Battle of Ushant. He sided with Keppel and testified against Sir Hugh Palliser, so he was stripped of command for the duration of the American War of Independence. Lord Sandwich convinced him to become Admiralty Commissioner in 1783, however, and he was promptly dispatched to lead the Mediterranean Fleet aboard HMS *Trusty*.

He then fell ill and returned to England to recuperate but he died in Marlborough in 1788 at the age of just 51. Such was his reputation that he was buried in Westminster Abbey.

ADMIRAL
THE VISCOUNT
AUGUSTUS KEPPEL

Keppel was *Victory*'s first commander. Born in 1725, he was the son Willem and Anne van Keppel (his mother descended from Charles II) and went to sea at the tender age of 10. In 1740, he joined Lord Anson on the *Centurion* and the pair sailed around the world for the next four years. His first command was the 50-gun fourth-rate ship-of-the-line HMS *Maidstone*, although he ran her aground while chasing a French frigate in 1747 and was lucky to be acquitted by court-martial.

He returned to sea as Commodore of the Mediterranean Fleet at the age of just 24 but was then transferred to North America during the Seven Years' War. His 74-gun ship *Torbay* was the first to see action at the Battle of Quiberon Bay in 1759 and he was part of the British force that took Havana in 1762. He was promptly promoted to rear-admiral, and then vice-admiral in 1770.

Keppel was the MP for Windsor between 1761 and 1780 but George III excluded the Whigs from power and he was given command of the Channel

Fleet instead. He was convinced Lord Sandwich, then the first lord of the admiralty and a powerful ally of the king, wanted him to be defeated by the French fleet. The navy was in a state of disrepair and the First Battle of Ushant exposed its weaknesses.

Keppel criticised Admiral Sir Hugh Palliser, who he deemed partly responsible for the navy's shortcomings, and the hostility between them eventually led to a series of scandals culminating in them both being court-martialled but later acquitted. Keppel was raised to the peerage in 1782 but he resigned from politics in protest at the Peace of Paris in 1783 and gradually faded from public life. He died in 1786.

CAPTAIN JOHN CAMPBELL

John Campbell was born in Dumfries, Scotland, in 1720. He worked for the master of a small coastal vessel as a boy and then volunteered for the navy. He served on three ships before joining the *Centurion* as a midshipman in 1740. *Centurion* became the flagship of Commodore George Anson and completed a circumnavigation of

FAR LEFT Lord Augustus Keppel in later life (by Sir Joshua Reynolds)

LEFT Captain John Campbell in 1782

the globe, after which Campbell was promoted to master.

With Anson fighting his corner, Campbell worked his way up the ranks and proved his worth by helping Astronomer Royal James Bradley perfect the art of celestial navigation. He then trialled new lunar tables and a reflecting circle before recommending the admiralty develop a more accurate sextant, the prototype of all modern instruments used today.

He soon joined the *Royal George* as flag captain and served under Admiral Edward Hawke at the Battle of Quiberon Bay in 1759. Hawke then dispatched Campbell and Anson to England to deliver news of their victory to the king. When peace broke out in 1763, Campbell was tasked with analysing the data from John Harrison's longitude watch but he was back at sea as commander of the royal yacht (*Royal Caroline*) within a year.

His career seemed to be winding down but then his old friend Augustus Keppel asked him to captain the Channel Fleet aboard HMS *Victory*. Campbell was in command at the First Battle of Ushant and would have pursued the fleeing French fleet had Sir Hugh Palliser followed orders, but Palliser neglected to ram home the English advantage and the battle was indecisive.

Campbell remained with *Victory* until the end of the year but he wasn't offered another command until Keppel succeeded Sandwich as the first sea lord four yours later. Having been appointed to HMS *Portland*, Campbell's fleet was intercepted by a Franco-Spanish force off Newfoundland. He managed to escape but the allied fleet embarrassed the English and captured 18 ships.

He retired to continue his navigational work and trialled Thomas Mudge's chronometer along with the Board of Longitude's achromatic telescope on another trip to North America. He died in London in 1790.

CAPTAIN JONATHAN FAULKNOR

Jonathan Faulknor was destined to join the navy: his grandfather commanded ships during the War of Spanish Succession in the first years of the 18th century, and his father was killed when the earlier incarnation of HMS *Victory* was lost in a storm in 1744. Two of his brothers captained ships in the Seven Years' War, and his nephew died while fighting a French frigate off Guadeloupe in 1795.

Jonathan was born in the 1730s and he rose through the naval ranks to become an officer by the end of the Seven Years' War. He commanded HMS *Furnace* as part of Commodore Keppel's fleet that saw action against the French off Senegal in 1758. The following year he was appointed post-captain of HMS *Mercury*. He spent the next three years patrolling the West Indies but was then without a command until he captained Rear-Admiral Sir John Moore's flagship HMS *Superb* in 1767. The ship ran aground off Cork but the pilot was to blame and Faulknor safely refloated her before taking into the dockyard for repairs.

He was left without a ship for the next seven years but returned to action as master of the 74-gun third-rate *Royal Oak*, which was assigned to patrol the English Channel. In 1778, he graduated to flag captain aboard the *Victory* and served under Keppel and Campbell at the Battle of Ushant in July. He performed admirably and was tasked with delivering news of the battle back to Britain.

He saw more action during the Siege of Gibraltar and the Battle of Cape Spartel, and he was promoted to flag rank in 1787. He spent the last years of his career in Havant and was about to be presented to King George III – having finally been promoted to admiral – when he collapsed and died of a stroke.

SIR FRANCIS GEARY AND RICHARD KEMPENFELT

Geary was born in Aberystwyth in 1709 but the family moved first to Shropshire and then to Buckinghamshire. He was a talented bell-ringer in his youth but he chose to join the navy in 1727 and initially served on HMS *Revenge* in the Baltic Campaign. Geary's early career was undistinguished and it took him 15 years to be promoted to lieutenant.

He took command of HMS *Squirrel* in 1742 and saw immediate action off Madeira where he captured two Spanish ships and a heavily laden French merchantman. Geary's career then took off as he captured another nine ships in the next two years. He then spent two more years aboard the 74-gun HMS *Culloden* patrolling the Bay of Biscay. When he returned to England he was promoted to commodore and commanded the

squadron in the Medway. In 1748 he relinquished the position and retired to the Polesden Lacey estate in rural Surrey.

He returned to service at the outbreak of the Seven Years' War in 1755 and took command of HMS *Somerset*. He captured several privateers and was promoted to rear-admiral aboard HMS *Resolution* in 1759. He then transferred his flag to HMS *Sandwich* but the ship was laid up after losing her mainmast in a storm and missed the Battle of Quiberon Bay. He prevented the French fleet from sailing to the East Indies in 1760 and returned to fly his flag aboard HMS *Royal Sovereign* as vice-admiral of the blue.

He retired again at the end of the war but was recalled for the second time as relations with Spain soured in 1769. Tensions eased immediately, however, so he retired again only to be recalled to active duty at the age of 71. Despite being in poor health, he raised his flag aboard HMS *Victory* and appointed Richard Kempenfelt as his captain. The pair took command of the Channel Fleet and immediately captured 12 enemy merchant ships off Brest.

He returned to Portsmouth in August 1780 and asked to be relieved of command. His request was granted and he spent his final years on his Surrey estate. He died in 1796 at the age of 86. Only one of his three children (his second son) survived him; his eldest son was killed in North America in 1776 and his daughter died two years later.

Richard Kempenfelt was born in London and joined the navy as a lieutenant in 1741 at the age of 22. He saw service immediately in the War of Jenkins' Ear but returned to England in 1746. The war, which lasted from 1739 until 1748, was given its unusual name after Robert Jenkins (captain of the merchant ship *Rebecca*) had his ear severed by Spanish boarders from the patrol boat *La Isabela*

off the Florida coast in 1731. The Spanish commander, Julio León Fandiño, told Jenkins to report the incident to his king and threatened to do the same to the monarch. Jenkins recounted the incident to Parliament in 1738 and the British deemed it such an insult that they declared war on Spain.

Kempenfelt was perhaps most famous for masterminding the victory over the Comte de Guichen's French fleet at the (second) Battle of Ushant in 1781. Kempenfelt was aboard the *Victory* when it attacked and captured 15 merchant ships of the French convoy before the escorts could intervene. When the escorts finally tried to engage,

LEFT Admiral Sir Francis Geary in Portsmouth

BELOW The medallion commemorating the loss of the Royal George

they were scattered by poor weather and had to return to port.

The following year, Kempenfelt was assigned to HMS *Royal George* as part of Lord Howe's fleet. The ship was due to help with the Siege of Gibraltar but she needed a minor refit in Portsmouth to make her seaworthy. As she was being heeled in the harbour to make repairs below the waterline, several of her cannon were moved inboard. Their weight fractured rotten timbers in the ship's frame and a sudden breeze then rolled the ship over. Kempenfelt was trapped in his cabin and died along with around 900 men, women and children who were also aboard.

ADMIRAL RICHARD HOWE

Richard Howe was born in London in 1726. He joined the navy at the age of 14 and went to Cape Horn with the South Seas Fleet under George Anson. He was promoted to lieutenant after the unsuccessful attack on La Guaira in the West Indies in 1743, and he then commanded the sloop *Baltimore* in the North Sea during the Jacobite Rebellion. He was seriously wounded during an engagement with French privateers but went on to captain several ships during the Seven Years' War.

Howe earned a reputation as a skilful and efficient captain and led the British fleet to victory at the Battle of Quiberon Bay. Having removed the threat of a French invasion of Britain, Howe became MP for Dartmouth and then joined the admiralty board as treasurer of the navy. He was eventually promoted to vice-admiral and commander-in-chief of the Mediterranean Fleet. He was a family friend of Benjamin Franklin so he tried to negotiate peace during the American War of Independence. He was unsuccessful and was tasked with upholding the blockade of North American ports instead.

He resigned his commission due to his sympathy with the colonists but was immediately called back into service when the French entered the war. Howe outmanoeuvred a superior enemy fleet at Sandy Hook and thwarted the Comte d'Estaing's attempts to capture Newport. Howe returned to England with a bitter distrust of a system that hadn't allowed him to broker peace talks or given him the necessary support for war.

He joined the opposition in Par-

LEFT Admiral of the Fleet Richard Howe (by John Singleton Copley)

liament and was therefore denied a commission but Lord Cornwallis's surrender at Yorktown undermined Lord North's government and it was eventually replaced by a weak coalition in 1782. Howe was immediately given command of HMS *Victory* and the Channel Fleet. His mission was to protect merchant ships arriving from North America; monitor the French, Spanish and Dutch fleets; and plan for relieving the city of Gibraltar, which had been under siege since 1779.

Howe outmanoeuvred the French off the Scilly Isles and ensured a vital trade convoy reached England. He then forced the Dutch fleet to remain in port before sailing for Gibraltar. His 33 ships again eluded the much larger French fleet and Howe finally delivered relief supplies to the rock in October 1782. Although he managed to keep the supply lines open to the colony, the indecisive Battle of Cape Spartel saw him forced back to England.

The Peace of Paris ended the conflict the following year and Howe was promoted to first lord of the admiralty. He oversaw the arms race with the French and Spanish, and also introduced changes to the outdated signalling sys-

tem. He was offered another commission when Britain and Spain almost went to war over Nootka Sound in the Pacific but the crisis was eventually resolved and he didn't see action again until the French Revolutionary War in 1794.

As commander of the Channel Fleet, Howe ordered a direct attack on the French fleet protecting an American grain ship. The merchantman managed to survive but Howe sank seven enemy ships and killed or captured 7,000 sailors. The tactical victory allowed Britain to maintain her blockade of French ports for the remainder of the war. Howe was hailed a hero and made Viscount of Langar and then Knight of the Order of the Garter. He died in London in 1799 but has since had four ships and numerous capes and islands named after him.

VICE-ADMIRAL SIR THOMAS HARDY

Thomas Hardy was born in Dorset in 1769 and he joined the navy aged only 12 as the captain's servant aboard HMS *Helena*. He returned to England in 1782 to complete his schooling and was then transferred between several fifth- and

LEFT The overwhelming British victory at the Battle of Quiberon Bay

sixth-rate ships in the Mediterranean before being promoted to second lieutenant in 1793. He became first lieutenant aboard HMS *Minerve* in 1796. Commodore Horatio Nelson moved his broad pennant to the *Minerve* later that year and thereafter the two men would be inextricably linked, first with *Victory* and then with Trafalgar.

Minerve and HMS *Blanche* captured the Spanish frigate *Santa Sabina* while en route to Gibraltar in December. They then ran into the main Spanish fleet and the *Minerve* was only saved when Hardy lured the Spanish into a chase. He fought until the captured ship was dis-masted and recaptured by the Spanish. Hardy survived the encounter and was exchanged for Don Jacobo Stuart, captain of the *Santa Sabina*. He rejoined *Minerve* in Gibraltar and was praised by Nelson again when he rescued a sailor who had fallen overboard while the Spanish were closing in.

Hardy was promoted to Captain of HMS *Mutine* and immediately saw action at the Battle of the Nile in August 1798. Nelson was so impressed with his seamanship that he promoted Hardy to captain of the fleet flagship, HMS *Vanguard*, after the decisive engagement that had largely destroyed the French fleet. Hardy oversaw the operation to evacuate Lady Hamilton's family from Naples to Sicily four months later and he eventually returned to England in 1799.

He became Nelson's flag captain once more when he took command of HMS *St George* in 1801. The pair joined the Baltic Fleet and Hardy was tasked with depth sounding the bay around the Danish fleet at Copenhagen. The water was too shallow so the *St George* couldn't join the battle the following day. The only two ships that ignored his soundings, HMS *Agamemnon* and HMS *Bellona*, both ran aground during the engagement.

Hardy was assigned to HMS *Amphion* in 1802, and Nelson joined him the following year when *Victory*'s repairs overran. When her £70,000 refit was finally complete, Hardy and Nelson transferred to the *Victory* off Toulon. Hardy was by now flag captain and unofficial captain of the entire fleet. He blockaded Toulon but the French fleet slipped through his grasp and escaped

to the West Indies in the spring of 1805.

Hardy and Nelson gave chase but they briefly returned home after an unsuccessful pursuit. They then headed for Cádiz to try to engage the French fleet once more. Trafalgar would also be Hardy's finest hour and perhaps the most overwhelming naval victory in history. As *Victory* approached the French fleet, she came under intense fire from the enemy broadsides. Hardy urged Nelson to take refuge on one of the ships in the rear squadron but Nelson refused to leave his side.

When a splinter struck Hardy in the foot, Nelson commented that the battle was getting too hot for his liking. Shortly afterwards, in the ensuing mêlée, Nelson was fatally wounded by a musket round fired from the *Redoutable*. Hardy helped carry Nelson below and remained with him for much of the remainder of the battle, although he couldn't neglect his duty as captain and repeatedly hurried topside to direct the battle.

Victory needed extensive repairs after Trafalgar but she finally sailed for home from Gibraltar in November. She arrived in Portsmouth a month later and Hardy carried one of the banners at

LEFT Vice-Admiral Thomas Hardy was with Nelson when he died

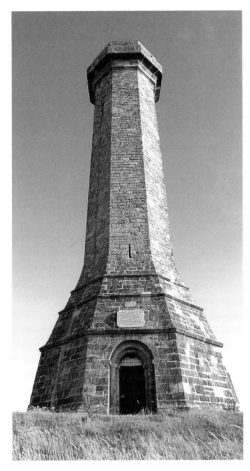

Nelson's funeral in January.

Hardy went on to command HMS *Triumph* and HMS *Ramillies* in North America. He captured Eastport but was then defeated at Stonington. He was promoted to commodore on his return to England and took command of the royal yacht, HMS *Princess Augusta*. He then became commander-in-chief of the South American squadron and helped protect Mexico, Colombia and Argentina from the Spanish.

Hardy was promoted to rear-admiral in 1825 and he immediately helped crush the Lisbon Rebellion. He resigned from the navy in 1834 and died three years later in Greenwich. A 22-metre monument was erected to his memory on Black Down Hill in Dorset in 1844. The monument is visible from 100 kilometres and has been used as a shipping landmark for more than 170 years, a fitting memorial for one of Britain's greatest mariners.

FAR LEFT Hardy's ship HMS St George

LEFT The Hardy Monument on Black Down Hill

ADMIRAL SAMUEL HOOD

Samuel Hood was born in Somerset in 1724. When he was 16, his father helped Captain Thomas Smith with his stranded carriage and then put him up for the night. The young Hood was inspired by Smith's stories from the high seas and joined the navy in 1741. He became a lieutenant five years later and saw active service in the North Sea. He was given his first command in 1754 and was promoted to post-captain of HMS *Grafton* at the outbreak of the Seven Years' War in 1756.

He immediately captured three French ships and destroyed several more transports in the raid on Le Havre in 1759. He became commander-in-chief of the North American Station in 1767 but returned to England three years later. He didn't receive his next commission until 1778 but it effectively signalled the end of his active career as it was with the naval academy. However, he was back on duty in the West Indies when the admiralty found itself short of experienced flag officers in the American Revolutionary War.

He acquitted himself well when driving the French from their anchorage on St Kitts and then helped defeat a Franco-Spanish fleet planning to invade Jamaica. During the conflict he met Horatio Nelson, then a young frigate commander. The two men formed a lasting friendship and Hood became something of a mentor to Nelson (the latter described Hood as 'the greatest sea officer I ever knew').

He became MP for Westminster during the peace that followed and he was eventually promoted to the admiralty board in 1788. From 1790 until August 1791, Hood raised his flag on HMS *Victory* but the ship saw little action. The following year, Hood presided over the trial of the mutineers from HMS *Bounty*. In 1793, he commanded the Mediterranean Fleet and occupied first Toulon and then Corsica.

He retired from the navy to serve as Governor of Greenwich Hospital while continuing his parliamentary duties. He was one of the chief mourners at Nelson's funeral in January 1806. Hood died a decade later. HMS *Hood* was named in his honour but the *Bismarck* sank the Royal Navy's last battlecruiser in May 1941.

LEFT Admiral Samuel Hood

ADMIRAL HYDE PARKER

Parker was born in Devon in 1739. He joined the navy at his father's behest (his father was Vice-Admiral Sir Hyde Parker) in his early teens and had graduated to the rank of lieutenant by 1758. He was given his first command, *Manila*, in 1762 and thereafter spent much of his career patrolling the West Indies. He also fought a superb offensive action in New York in 1776, which earned him a knighthood. His ship was wrecked off Cuba in 1778 but his crew held out against the natives until they were rescued. Parker then fought alongside his father at the Battle of Dogger Bank and with Lord Howe in two sea battles off Gibraltar.

Parker was promoted to rear-admiral when England declared war on the French in 1793. He immediately raised his flag on HMS *Victory* and

LEFT Hood presided over the trial of the Bounty mutineers

ABOVE Admiral Sir Hyde Parker

served under Admiral Hood in the Mediterranean, but he then shifted his attention back to the West Indies. Having been promoted to admiral in 1799, he was then given command of the fleet tasked with taking Copenhagen two years later. Most of Parker's ships were too big to enter the shallow channel so he sent his second-in-command to fight the battle. Vice-Admiral Horatio Nelson

ignored his signal to disengage when it appeared English losses would precede defeat, and Danish forces eventually succumbed to superior seamanship.

Parker was then criticised for not routing the retreating fleet. He returned to England and was succeeded by Nelson, the latter praising him for being "as good a subject as His Majesty has". Parker died in 1807.

ADMIRAL SIR JOHN JERVIS

Jervis was born in the Midlands in 1735 to Swynfen and Elizabeth. His father worked for the admiralty and wanted his son to become a barrister. John went to Burton Grammar School but then ran away from Reverend Swindon's Academy in London to join the navy at the age of just 13. He was eventually persuaded to return home but Admiral George Townsend convinced the family to let him take Jervis aboard HMS *Gloucester* as an able seaman. He then saw active service against Spanish and French privateers along the Mosquito Coast.

In 1754 he transferred to the *Sphinx* as a midshipman and then returned to England to serve under John Campbell on the royal yacht *William & Mary*. When he passed his exams in March the following year, he was assigned to the mighty *Royal George* and then the 60-gun *Nottingham*. He transferred between several more ships before being given his first command, albeit temporarily, of HMS *Experiment*. While aboard HMS *Porcupine*, he and James Cook led armed transports upriver past Quebec. He then travelled extensively throughout North America, the Mediterranean, Europe and Russia.

During his time abroad, Jervis kept detailed notes on every harbour, defensive installation and anchorage so he could improve the admiralty's charts.

ABOVE Sir John Jervis

These would prove invaluable to later generations of seafarers. He then served under Keppel as captain of the *Foudroyant* at the Battle of Ushant, and was later called to give evidence that helped clear Keppel at his court-martial. He returned to the ship to help with the relief of Gibraltar but was wounded during the battle for the French ship *Pégase* on the way home. The French ship eventually struck her colours and Jervis was invested as a Knight of the Bath.

He also fought at the Battle of Cape Spartel but his next orders – negotiate peace in the West Indies – were rescinded at the end of the war in 1783. He used his downtime to run for office and became MP for Launceston but he was recalled to the navy during the Nootka Sound Crisis that threatened to descend into war with Spain. The incident was resolved peaceably but he was soon back on active service in the Caribbean during the Napoleonic Wars.

He then took command of the Mediterranean Fleet and used HMS *Victory* as his flagship. He counted among his subordinates Nelson and Cuthbert Collingwood. He enforced strict codes of discipline, exercise and hygiene and improved the health – and therefore fighting efficiency – of his sailors. This was a time when mutiny due to officer cruelty, low pay and poor conditions was common, so Jervis tightened up shipboard routine and introduced new rules to deal with unruly crews, which occasionally meant trying and executing them on consecutive days. However, he also ensured that they never ran out of tobacco or rum, and insisted that their post be delivered on time. He also once reimbursed a sailor who had lost his life savings after falling overboard with the cash in his pockets.

The Spanish and French gradually forced the British out of the Mediterranean, however. Having retreated to Gibraltar, Jervis's fleet of 15 ships-of-the-line was ambushed by 31 Spanish ships off Cape St Vincent on Valentine's Day 1797. Nelson on HMS *Captain* disobeyed Jervis's orders and attacked the Spanish immediately, capturing two ships singlehandedly. Another two were captured during the mêlée, although Jervis decided to repair his own ships rather than rout the fleeing Spanish. He was still feted as a military hero and awarded the title of Earl St Vincent. Nelson was invested as Knight of the Bath for his contribution.

By 1799, Jervis's health was failing so

he relinquished his command and returned to Essex to live out retirement with his wife. His health gradually improved, however, so he once again assumed command of the Channel Fleet. Two years later, he vowed to eliminate the corruption that was rife in Britain's dockyards so he was constantly at loggerheads with the admiralty. He eventually established the Commission of Inquiry and began the lengthy process of modernising the navy.

He didn't resume active service until shortly after Trafalgar, although by then he was 70 and he spent more time ashore than with HMS *Hibernia*. He was constantly frustrated by the navy's tradition of promoting sailors based on social standing rather than competence. When he finally retired in 1807, he told the king that this issue had to be addressed if the navy were to maintain its dominance over the French and Spanish. He then set about donating large sums of money to the wounded from Waterloo and other conflicts.

He died in 1823 and was buried in Staffordshire, his contribution to the way the navy performed at home and in battle incalculable. Five ships and myriad geographical features have since been named in his honour.

Design & Artwork: ALEX YOUNG

Published by: DEMAND MEDIA LIMITED

Publisher: JASON FENWICK

Written by: LIAM McCANN